To Mary

from

Max

EIGHT
QUESTIONS
PEOPLE
ASK
ABOUT
JUDAISM

EIGHT
QUESTIONS
PEOPLE
ASK
ABOUT
JUDAISM

by Dennis Prager & Joseph Telushkin

Tze Ulmad Press

Tze Ulmad Press

1101 Peppertree Lane
Simi Valley, California 93064

Library of Congress Catalog Number: 75-2969

Printed in the United States of America

First Edition
Sixth Printing—April 1977

For Our Parents
Max and Hilda Prager
Shlomo and Helen Telushkin
*who provided environments conducive
to asking questions and seeking
answers.*

PREFACE

We have written this book because we are convinced that when people understand Judaism, they will take it seriously.

*　　*　　*

Eight Questions People Ask About Judaism is both an introduction to Judaism and an inquiry into its relevance and meaning. It is our hope that people from every background, Jew or Gentile, religious or atheist, will read and be challenged by this book.

This book is only a first statement, and given our relative youth, we certainly hope to eventually further develop some of our views. But we could not wait ten or twenty years to write this book. Every day more of our contemporaries cut their roots to Judaism—and for only one reason: ignorance.

For eleven years we have struggled with questions such as these eight; and for the last three years, we have offered some of these eight answers to the North American Jewish community. The response has been so intense that writing this book became for us a compulsion. We only hope that our efforts to communicate the power of Judaism will bear fruits. "It is not for you to finish the task," the Talmud tells us, "but neither are you free to abandon it."

*　　*　　*

We are grateful to many individuals with whom we have discussed Judaism and related issues over the years. To name all of them is impossible, but we do wish to cite a few names which we recall with particular gratitude: Dr. Shlomo Bardin, Rabbi Saul Berman, Rabbi David Eliach,

Rabbi Norman Frimer, Rabbi Irving Greenberg, Rabbi Robert Hirt, Rabbi Steven Riskin, Rabbi Avraham Weiss, and though we have never met him, Rabbi Eliezer Berkovits, whose courageous books and articles have served as a beacon in the general darkness of the post-Auschwitz era.

We are also deeply appreciative of the suggestions and criticisms offered to us by Dr. Howard Siegel, Shalva Siegel, Dr. Steven M. Cohen and Jerry Unterman. We are especially indebted to Jon Groner for his incisive stylistic advice.

We wish to thank Ed Goldstein, Henry Kuhn, and the other wonderful people at the Mod Komp Corporation whose professionalism in typesetting this book was superseded only by their generosity; Theresa Catuogno for her cooperation and expertise in typing; and Cynthia Dachowitz whose energy and enthusiasm kept Tze Ulmad Institute functioning in its difficult beginning days.

Finally, we say thank you from the depths of our souls to those Jews in each community whose commitment to Judaism and the Jewish people has served as our single greatest source of inspiration.

Dennis Prager and Joseph Telushkin
Whitestone, New York
February, 1975

CONTENTS

EIGHT QUESTIONS
PEOPLE ASK
ABOUT JUDAISM

Question 1

CAN ONE DOUBT GOD'S EXISTENCE AND STILL BE A GOOD JEW?

IS BELIEF IN GOD RATIONAL?

WHAT IF I CANNOT BELIEVE?

God may have His own reasons for denying us certainty with regard to His existence and nature. One reason apparent to us that man's certainty with regard to anything is poison to his soul. Who knows this better than moderns who have had to cope with dogmatic Fascists, Communists and even scientists?

Emanuel Rackman, *The Condition of Jewish Belief*

. . . even if evil were a total mystery on which theology could not so much as make a dent, the God-faith would still be indicated. For, at the worst, it leaves less unexplained than does its alternative. If the believer has his troubles with evil, the atheist has more and graver difficulties to contend with. Reality stumps him altogether, leaving him baffled not by one consideration but by many, from the existence of natural law through the instinctual cunning of the insect to the brain of the genius and heart of the prophet. This then is the intellectual reason for believing in God: That, though this belief is not free from difficulties, it stands out, head and shoulders, as the best answer to the riddle of the universe.

Milton Steinberg, *Anatomy of Faith*

1

Does God exist? This is the most crucial question facing man. The implications of the conclusion have the most significant consequences for the meaning of human existence.

Yet, despite its overwhelming importance, serious and dispassionate discussion of God is usually confined to a handful of theologians and philosophers. The rest of us form simple opinions of belief, agnosticism, or atheism at a relatively early age and are content to retain them without questioning for the rest of our lives.

We must therefore begin our presentation of Judaism with a discussion about God. First, let us briefly note Judaism's attitude towards a most common contemporary sentiment about God: doubt.

CAN ONE DOUBT GOD'S EXISTENCE AND STILL BE A GOOD JEW?

Yes.

There are two significant reasons why your doubts about the existence of God should be no obstacle to your becoming or remaining a good Jew.

1. JUDAISM'S ESSENCE: DEED MORE THAN CREED

Doubt about the existence of God is no reason to deny Judaism as a way of life. Despite its ultimate goal of bringing mankind to the recognition of God and His universal moral law, Judaism stresses action far more than faith. The Talmud attributes to God a declaration which is probably unique among religious writings: "Better that they (the Children of Israel) abandon Me, but follow My laws" (for, the Talmud adds, through living by My laws they will come to Me, *Jerusalem Talmud Haggigah* 1:7). Thus, according to Judaism, one can be a good Jew while doubt-

ing God's existence, so long as he or she observes the
Jewish laws, but the converse is not true, for one who
believes in God but abandons Jewish law cannot be considered a good Jew.

It is not of course our intention to show that God is not
central to Judaism, merely to emphasize that the value and
excellence of Judaism can be appreciated and enacted inde-
pendently of one's present level of belief in God. One should
incorporate Judaism's ideals into one's daily life by studying and practicing Judaism even while one doubts God's
existence, because Jewish study and practice have moral
and spiritual benefits in and of themselves.

The basic Jewish view on this issue, and one which our
experience has confirmed, is that once one has begun to
study and live Judaism (see Questions 2 & 8), he or she will
conclude that God is the ultimate source of Judaism, morality, and life. In the words of the Talmud: "Whereas one
may [begin to] practice Judaism for non-divine reasons
[such as habit or a rational or ethical conviction], he eventually will do so convinced that it represents God's will"
(*Pesahim* 50b).

2. GOD DOES NOT WISH CERTAINTY
WITH REGARD TO HIS EXISTENCE

Belief in God is not always easy. Therefore, crises of
faith are to be expected, and the admission of such crises is
in no way an irreligious act for a religious Jew. As to why
God has denied man absolute certainty with regard to His
existence two answers suggest themselves.

a) In order for the human being to act morally, he must
have freedom of choice. Freedom to choose good (i.e., obedience to God's will) or evil (i.e., disobedience to God)
would be severely curtailed if we had absolute certainty of
God's existence.

b) *Absolute certainty leads to fanaticism.* As Emanuel

Rackman, a prominent Orthodox rabbi, has written: "Judaism encourages doubt even as it enjoins faith and commitment. A Jew dare not live with absolute certainty, because certainty is the hallmark of the fanatic and Judaism abhors fanaticism, [and] because doubt is good for the human soul, its humility . . . God may have had His own reasons for denying us certainty with regard to His existence and nature. One apparent reason is that man's certainty with regard to anything is poison to his soul. Who knows this better than moderns who have had to cope with dogmatic Fascists, Communists, and even scientists?" (*The Condition of Jewish Belief*, New York: 1969, p. 179).

Thus, doubts concerning God are no barrier to Jewish commitment. But, the doubter will argue, belief in God is not rational.

IS BELIEF IN GOD RATIONAL?

Does God exist?

God cannot be known to exist as one can know that a table or a cat exists. Their existences can be empirically proven. But God's existence cannot be empirically proven since by definition God possesses no physical qualities. *One can prove the existence of the natural, the physical, the finite; God, however, is supernatural, metaphysical, infinite.* Therefore, the question of proving God's existence is utterly irrelevant to God's existence since the only thing the impossibility of proving God's existence proves is that God is not physical, a position that Judaism has always maintained.*

---

*The third of Maimonides' Thirteen Principles of the Jewish Faith is that God has no physical qualities. Cf. *Deuteronomy* 4:12.

On the other hand, God's existence cannot be disproven either. Therefore, attempts to prove or disprove the existence of something which has never offered itself as provable are, to put it succinctly, a waste of time.

However, attempts to show through reason, logic, and human experience why God's existence is probable or improbable and why belief in God is beneficial or harmful are not at all a waste of time. The implications of the conclusions as they relate to truth, morality, and the ultimate meaning of life are of such unique significance that enlightened discussion about God should be welcomed by all people who seek truth, meaning, and a more moral world.*

We wish therefore, to advance certain arguments, though by no means all there are, which render the existence of God rationally probable and morally indispensable.

GOD'S EXISTENCE: RATIONALLY PROBABLE

First, let us borrow an idea from Milton Steinberg: *The believer in God must explain one thing, the existence of suffering; the non-believer, however, must explain the existence of everything else.*

The most frequently offered argument against belief in God is the existence of evil in the world. If God exists, we are asked and we ask ourselves, how do we account for the existence of so much evil?

This is certainly a difficult and terribly disturbing ques-

---

*The converse is also true. Ideologies or regimes that forbid people the right to discuss the issue of God seek neither truth nor a more moral world, but only the acquisition or retention of their own power. Contemporary examples are Communist regimes which forbid pro-religious advocacy. In the Soviet Union, for example, it is a crime to advocate the existence of God. See also the discussion on Marxism and Judaism in Question 4, part 2.

tion, and we will deal with it. Let us first, however, counter this question with one to the non-believer. If there is *no* God, how do you account for the existence of all that is good in the world? For consciousness and conscience? intelligence? emotions? love? the laws of nature? the sense of purpose which pervades organisms from the ant to the human being? all creation?

Those of us who affirm God's existence see such nonphysical phenomena as manifestations of a transcendent Being. How does the atheist account for all these phenomena? Generally, the atheist will explain, they have developed through a coincidence of molecules or the random couplings of gases and chemicals. In sum, *everything*, according to the atheist, developed by chance.*

We admit that it is possible that good, pleasure, beauty, love, art, intelligence, consciousness, conscience, natural laws, cellular activity, the pervasive sense of purpose, and all creation emanated from inanimate coincidences. But while we must entertain this as a possibility, *logic and reason* compel us to reject it as a probability. Infinitely more logical to us is the probability that everything emanates from a transcendent Being, for *design suggests to us a Designer, law a Lawgiver, creation a Creator, intelligence a Source of intelligence, conscience God.*

We therefore submit to the reader the two possibilities: creation from coincidence and chance or creation from design and purpose. Or, to put it another way, *the choice is*

*Even if the atheist claims that he has no specific answers to explain the origins of these phenomena, but that one day science will give us these answers, this answer still ascribes everything to chance, since he is maintaining that impersonal random forces constitute the ultimate cause of good, pleasure, consciousness, conscience, intelligence, and so on. Now science will undoubtedly supply us with more information, but science describes only *techniques*, and techniques have no relevance to the questions of who or what is behind these techniques, or *for what purpose* these techniques and life in general exist.

between nonsense and sense. If there is no God, one cannot
speak of sense in life, or of good and evil, or of ultimate
purpose, for these things would then be mere delusions
created by our minds to deny the reality that all is anarchic
and meaningless. If there is no God, nothing but the physical is real; all else are imaginings. Thus, if you posit that
there is no God, you must accept the fact that everything
you feel or to which you ascribe any meaning (such as good
and evil) is a delusion.*

But the moment you affirm that any non-physical quality
is real rather than a delusion, you are affirming the existence of God. From where else but God do these non-
physical realities derive? Gases and amino acids do not
possess truth, moral awareness, self-consciousness, a sense
of purpose, or other such non-physical qualities. Without
God, all of existence is a purposeless chance arrangement
of molecules. For this reason among others, we say that
God's existence is logically and rationally probable. Logic
and reason suggest to us that non-physical phenomena
(goodness, justice, love, etc.) are not delusions, but constitute an objective reality which reflect their only possible
source, the ultimate reality—God.

GOD'S EXISTENCE:
MORALLY INDISPENSABLE

If there is no God, the most significant aspect of life
which must be recognized as a delusion is morality, the

---

*This helps to explain why many Western individuals who do not
believe that God exists are attracted to one or more of the following
ways of life: a) hedonism (only pleasure is real); b) nihilism (no values are
real); c) Communism and Fascism (religion and meaning without God); d)
Eastern religions (reality is a delusion); e) moral relativism (morality is
not real but a matter of personal opinion or taste).

notion of right and wrong which transcends an individual's personal inclinations. Gases, acids, and molecules are not "right" or "wrong," or "good" or "evil." If matter is the one reality, right and wrong, i.e., morality, possess no reality. They are either popular opinions (at best), or objectively meaningless terms which represent no reality. Thus, it is a self-evident truism that if God does not exist, neither can morality. Without God, all we can have are *opinions* about what is morally "right" or "wrong."

It should be obvious, therefore, why in secular societies (as epitomized, for example, by many Western universities), morality is generally considered to be a matter of opinion. Moral relativism is the only possible consequence of the denial of God's existence; but this of course means that morality is nothing more than a personal opinion. As this century's most eloquent atheist philosopher, Bertrand Russell, wrote: "I cannot see how to refute the arguments for the subjectivity of ethical values *but*," *Russell conceded, "I find myself incapable of believing that all that is wrong with wanton cruelty is that I don't like it."*

Russell's second point is our whole point. All that can possibly be wrong with wanton cruelty according to atheism and its moral relativism, is that some individuals may personally not like it. *Amorality is, therefore, inherent to atheism.* *

To cite an example, if there is no God, by what standard was Hitler wrong? To the atheist and moral relativist, the only thing wrong with Nazi atrocities, as Russell said, "is that I don't like it."

---

*Amorality means, of course, no morality, not immorality. Thus, we recognize that good atheists can and do exist, and that atheists can have moral opinions, but they are good *despite*, not because of, their atheism (or atheist humanism—see Question 3, part 2 and Question 4, part 3).

One may answer that we know "deep down" that Hitler's mass murder and torture was wrong. But from where does this "deep down" recognition of right and wrong come? If there is no God, such feelings are just feelings, and moral *standards* cannot be based on *feelings*. But if indeed we all do possess natural "deep down" knowledge of good and evil, this fact can only point to some ultimately moral Being having put it within us.

Or, one may answer that mass murder is wrong for pragmatic reasons—the argument that "if we kill them, they'll start to kill us and the world will fall apart." But of course this is not a moral argument, and in any case, committing evil can be regarded as highly practical. As Lenin said, referring to the elimination of his opponents, "to make omelettes you've got to break eggs."

Or, one may answer that *reason* tells us that Hitler was wrong, that evil is wrong. Reason, according to this common attitude (see Question 4, part 3), suffices to lead us to moral behavior without the necessity of positing the existence of God. But is this so?

DOES REASON LEAD TO
OR DICTATE MORAL BEHAVIOR?

1. REASON MAY OR MAY NOT
LEAD TO MORALITY

Reason does not necessarily tell one to act morally. On the contrary, reason can always be used to justify immoral behavior—from the death camps of the Nazis to petty cheating in every day life. *The use of reason to justify what is wrong is so common that we have a special word for it—rationalization.*

Adolph Eichmann and other Nazi murderers acted quite

reasonably in not refusing orders and thereby endangering their careers. Indeed it may be persuasively argued that among the only people in Nazi Germany who acted *against* reason were those Germans who risked their lives in opposing Nazi barbarity.

To cite a common example, one out of every three American hotel guests steals something from his room. Since it is probable that most of these people consider stealing wrong, are we to assume that millions of Americans think of themselves as thieves? No. Undoubtedly these people *rationalize* their action by claiming that the hotel overcharged its guests, or that everyone else takes "souvenirs," or that the towel (or ashtray, or painting) will not be missed, etc.

Reason, in sum, *is amoral*. It is a human tool which can be used for evil just as easily as for good.

2. REASON CANNOT COMPEL MORAL BEHAVIOR

It should be obvious from the above examples that if reason can justify immorality, it cannot possibly be relied upon to compel morality. For even when reason does not justify immoral behavior, it is not reason which compels a person to act morally. Though reason may have suggested to a handful of Germans to actively oppose Nazism and to a majority of Americans not to steal from their hotel rooms it would be foolish to presume that it was reason which compelled them to act thus. Rather it was a recognition of a *morality transcending reason* which guided their actions.

Thus, given these two facts, that reason is amoral and that reason cannot compel moral behavior even when it might suggest it, one can accurately characterize the notion that reason alone can or will produce moral behavior as a myth—albeit a myth with wide intellectual support (see p. 101f.).

RELIANCE ON REASON VS.
MORAL RELATIVISM

The ultimate breakdown of the secular moral system occurs when, as is very often the case, this myth of reason leading to morality is held alongside the previously discussed myth of moral relativism leading to morality. For not only are both notions untenable in and of themselves, they also contradict one another! *If morality is a matter of opinion, reason becomes irrelevant.*

When right and wrong are regarded as matters of personal opinion, no single standard of morality exists; and when no one standard exists of what use is reason? Reason is of use only when it can be utilized to discover facts or to implement laws which exist independent of one's reason (just as, for example, if I am lost in a cave and am using reason to find an exit, reason will be of use to me in finding an exit only if an exit exists). Reason does not create facts or laws of science, it discovers and implements them. So, *too, reason can discover laws of morality; it cannot create them.*

In the realm of morality, therefore, reason and relativism are mutually contradictory. One must either recognize that one moral standard exists, in which case morality is not a matter of personal opinion (and then reason can be used to discover it); or, if one continues to hold that morality is relative, it must be acknowledged that reason is ultimately useless since morality does not exist (and reason then points to nothing conclusive).

When morality is relative, morality does not exist and reason is irrelevant because a) reason can justify any moral behavior, b) two equally rational opinions that conflict are equally valid, and c) the opinion of a less rational person is as valid as the opinion of a more rational one. If morality is a matter of personal preference, reason could no more determine whether an action is good or bad than it could determine if a certain ice cream flavor were good or bad.

WHAT IF I CANNOT BELIEVE?

Atheism

Atheism, then, is rationally no more (and apparently a good deal less) convincing an answer to the mysteries of human existence and the universe than is belief in God. On this issue, Voltaire, himself an unrelenting antagonist of organized religion, said: "In the opinion that there is a God, there are difficulties; but in the contrary opinion there are absurdities."

But atheism not only suffers from irrationality and amorality; it is for most of its adherents an intellectually lazy doctrine as well. Despite the fact that to many people atheism is usually associated with intellect, the fact is that the majority of atheists have no more questioned their beliefs than the most simple believers have questioned theirs. We will now more fully develop this point as we analyze the five categories into which atheists may be classified.

I Atheists who deny God because God was presented to them in a childish or superstitious manner.

It is an unfortunate but undeniable fact that God is often perceived and therefore presented in a foolish and distorted manner. A typical example is the anthropomorphic conception of God which portrays Him as, for example, a grand old man sitting up in heaven. Such a straw-man God is a likely target for atheists' jibes at believers; it was this caricature which Soviet cosmonauts mocked when they boasted that up in space they saw no God.

A second extremely common distortion is the portrayal of God as little more than some cosmic teddy-bear— someone for us to cling to when we are lonely or afraid, someone whose reason for being is to serve us rather than we Him. This misconception and simplification of God's essence is particularly common in the Western world.

The third and worst distortion of God takes place when evil is committed in His name. This is a favorite theme of atheists who point to Church atrocities as examples of the moral irrelevance of God. This argument, however, poses no problem to Judaism since it never claimed that faith in God alone produces good people or a good world. God is the basis of morality, but in order to achieve the Jewish goal of perfecting the world under the rule of God (see Question 5) two other emphases *must* accompany belief in God: the commitment to perfect this world, and the commitment of each individual to perfect him or herself, (see Question 2 and Question 4, part I).*

Moreover, if we are to negate the existence of God because certain individuals or groups have committed evil in God's name, then we must likewise negate the existence of, or need for, laws, science, sex, and any other noble goal or fact of life. Laws can put criminals in prison, but they can also, as in Nazi Germany and the Soviet Union, put criminals in power. Science can cure millions, but it can also

---

*Considering the fact that the Jews suffered the greatest atrocities at the hands of the Church throughout the latter's history, one would think that this argument should appeal to Jews more than anyone else. Obviously it has not; the fact that their torturers spoke of God made no impression on martyred Jews whatsoever. It only served to reconfirm the urgency of the Jewish role in the world.

destroy millions. Sex can be beautiful, but there are rapists. The fact that men can pervert the name of God, or corrupt laws, science, and sex only bears witness to the human potential to corrupt. Because we can pervert moral ideals does not mean we can do without them.

Therefore we invite the atheist who identifies himself in this category to examine the conception of God held in Jewish sources. After all, it was Judaism which brought God to the world. He will soon discover that anthropomorphic or teddy-bear conceptions of God are utterly foreign to Judaism. When Moses confronted God, he asked Him His name, "I am what I am," God replied. The Jew cannot know what God is, only *that He is* and *what He wants*.

II Atheists who deny God in rebellion against their home, background, parents, or external authority in general

This atheist is often related to the previous one. In addition to rejecting many other irrational practices and attitudes of their parents, this atheist often rejects the irrational religion or God of his parents. The rejection of a parent's religion or God is a very common aspect of many children's emotional or psychological rebellion against their homes.

Nor is this rejection of God limited to the children of authoritarian homes; it is equally true of children from overly permissive homes. For the children of very lenient parents, a very common pattern in Jewish homes of the past generation, are also quite likely to revolt against external authority. The children to whom parents gave "everything" came to see *themselves* as gods, thus owing nothing to any higher authority—be it a parent, a school, a government, or God.

III Atheists who deny God because they were raised in and/or live in a non-believing environment

Though few atheists may admit it, many of them hold views concerning God and religion which they learned from home and which they have rarely if ever questioned. Atheists rightly dismiss the beliefs of many religious individuals as little more than ingrained attitudes derived from the home or social environment. Atheists who have not sought to confront intelligent believers and their arguments, and who have not tested their denials of God in living situations among sophisticated religious people, are subject to the same criticism and dismissal.

Therefore the atheist who seeks truth, a better self and a better world is obligated to seek out religious people and religious literature before locking himself into atheist dogma. Intellectual honesty and moral concern demand this approach.

IV Atheists who deny God because of personal suffering or human suffering in general

There is not much which we can say to someone who denies the existence of God because of personal tragedy such as the death or suffering of loved ones. To these people we must offer an extended hand, not arguments.

Yet as understandable as is the denial of God's existence after personal tragedy, this denial constitutes an emotional rather than a rational response to the question of God. Our periods of suffering do not disprove God's existence any more than our moments of joy prove it.

Moreover, we must be specific when speaking of human suffering. There are two causes, man and nature, and the first reflects in no way upon the issue of God's existence.

MAN-MADE EVIL

Let us take a most terrible problem. faith after Auschwitz. How can we believe in God after He allowed six million Jews, including over a million little children, to be gassed, burned, experimented on, frozen, and transformed into soap bars and lamp shades? There is virtually no Jew who has not asked this question.

Before offering some thoughts on this question, a personal note is in order. Though both of us were born in the United States and after the Holocaust, and though neither of us lost any immediate relatives in the Holocaust, the Holocaust is the single greatest influence on our thinking. We can say without the least exaggeration that a part of each of us died with the six million.

Nevertheless, the Holocaust does not constitute an insurmountable obstacle to belief in God. First, God did not build Auschwitz and its crematoria. Men did. Man, not God, is responsible for the Holocaust. Judaism posits that man has freedom of choice. Perhaps we would prefer had men been created as robots who could do only good rather than as human beings capable of good and evil. But this is impossible; only where there exists the possibility of evil does there exist the possibility of good.

Second, it is morally unjustifiable and historically inaccurate to attribute the establishment of Israel to the Holocaust, but while the Holocaust may suggest to us Jews denial of God, to what do we attribute the survival of the Jewish people and the rise of Israel?

Third, *the Holocaust may make faith in God difficult; but it makes faith in man impossible.* Along with six million Jews, and tens of millions of others murdered by the Nazis and Communists, we must bury the doctrine which enabled Communism and Nazism to rise: the belief that man is God. After Auschwitz and Gulag Archipelago, we have two choices: belief in man under God or belief in nothing.

Thus, the question to be posed after Auschwitz, Gulag Archipelago, and other such barbarities is not "Where was God?" but "Where is man?"

NATURAL SUFFERING

With natural suffering (disease, earthquakes, etc.) we face a far more difficult problem than with man-made suffering. The latter we blame on men; but does it not seem logical to either blame or deny God because of natural suffering?

Before analyzing this problem let us note one fact concerning natural suffering.

Though natural suffering has always existed, man does have the capacity to greatly limit it, and in some cases, even to eliminate it. Man must therefore share part of the responsibility for the prevalence of natural suffering. If we spent as much money on research and preventive health measures as we have spent on cosmetics, let alone space exploration or defense, the decrease in human suffering would be substantial.

This consideration notwithstanding, we readily admit that the issue of natural suffering is the most difficult one confronting the believer in God. We would never claim to have a full answer to why God allows (or perhaps even ordains) natural suffering. This is a question which is by definition unanswerable. For if we define God as infinite and above nature, man, who is finite and within nature, cannot possibly understand all of God's ways. Three words of a medieval Hebrew philosopher sum up this truism: *lu yadativ hayitiv*, If I knew Him (God) I'd be Him.

This does not mean, however, that Judaism is silent on the issue of natural suffering. In fact, an entire book of the Bible, *Job*, is devoted to this issue. *Job* recounts the terrible sufferings endured by a man whom the Bible emphasizes was a particularly good and righteous man (thereby making the question of his suffering even sharper), and it details the questions and explanations offered by Job and his friends concerning human suffering and God. The Book of *Job* asks: why do good people suffer?

Job's friends are of the opinion that Job's (i.e., all men's) suffering is punishment for his sins. The Bible, i.e., Judaism, categorically rejects this notion.

Why then do men suffer? After 37 tense chapters of questioning and challenging, of bitterness and tears, God gives Job, and us, His answer:

> *Then God answered Job . . . and said:*
> *"Who is this that complicates ideas*
> *With words without knowledge?*
> *Get prepared like a man,*
> *I will ask you and you tell me.*
> *Where were you when I established the world?*
> *Tell me, if you know so much.*
> *Who drafted its dimensions? Do you know?*
> *Did you ever command forth a morning?*
> *Have death's gates been revealed to you?*
> *Have you examined earth's expanse?*
> *Tell me, if you know.*
> *Can you . . . guide the bear with her cubs?*
> *Does the hawk soar by your wisdom?*
> *Does the eagle mount at your command,*
> *And make his nest on high?"*
> *God answered Job and said:*
> *"Will the contender with God yield?*
> *He who reproves God, let him answer for it."*

Job answered God and said:
"Lo, I am small, how can I answer you?
My hand I lay on my mouth.
I have spoken once, I will not reply . . .
I talked of things I did not know,
Wonders beyond my ken . . ."

God's answer? God is God and who are we to assume that we can understand everything? Who "established the world"—we or God? Admittedly, this may not be the answer we hoped for, but *what answer would we desire?* If God is God and man is man, is there any other possible answer than the one given to Job?

Certainly Judaism could have presented a more "popular" image of God, or denied the reality of suffering (as was done often in the East), or theologically explained human suffering as divinely ordained punishment, but it did not do so.

To the rational and thinking person, this very honesty of Judaism, its unwillingness to compromise on the nature of God, despite its desire to gain adherents, is very reassuring. For we can affirm the existence of God without suspending either our reason or our questioning. On the contrary, for the Jew, reason and questioning should ultimately be a source of affirmation that there is a God; that He does care; and that ultimately there is meaning to my life—and yes, even to my suffering.

V Atheists who deny God because they have explored both sides of the issue

There remains a very small minority of atheists who do not fall into the first four categories. These individuals have come to the conclusion that there is no God, neither out of blind acceptance of an atheistic doctrine handed down to them, nor out of rebellion against home and environment, nor because God has been presented to them foolishly, nor out of an emotional reaction to tragedy, but after extensive efforts to believe, after reading intelligent presentations of the concept of God, and after sustained dialogue with sophisticated believers.

Frankly, we have never met such an individual, but we are aware of the existence of such individuals as Albert Camus. Yet, even these few extraordinary atheists must still account for the existence of everything other than suffering; and most important, they must still confront the greatest challenge to atheism: the relativization and resultant denial of morality which accompanies the denial of God. Atheism denies God, but what does it affirm?

God or god?

The answer is, of course, that atheism affirms nothing—though this does not mean that atheists affirm nothing. On the contrary, atheists replace God with gods of their own: man, reason, flags, ideologies, economic classes, 'progress,' revolution, culture, education, pleasure . . . The issue therefore is not belief or non-belief, but belief in God or belief in other gods.

At great cost in human life, however, we have learned that all these other gods have failed; that *without God each of these gods is meaningless and ultimately terribly dangerous* because they become ends in themselves, thereby justifying any means to their achievement.

For these reasons and others outlined in this chapter and in the remainder of the book, you are challenged to begin incorporating Judaism into your life, even as you continue to question God. For if you allow your doubts to justify non-compliance with Judaism, in what *practical* sense are you any different from the atheist? *You may be an agnostic in theory, but in practice you are either a believer or an atheist.* You must, therefore, make a conscious choice between God or gods, since even if you decide not to choose, a choice will have been made—but by your habits, ignorance, and laziness, rather than by your mind.

Question 2

WHY DO WE NEED ORGANIZED RELIGION? ISN'T IT ENOUGH TO BE AN ETHICAL PERSON?

WHO NEEDS JEWISH LAW—WILL OBSERVING THE SABBATH OR KEEPING KOSHER MAKE ME A BETTER PERSON?

. . . the purpose of the laws of the Torah is to promote compassion, loving-kindness and peace in the world.
> Moses Maimonides, *Yad Hazakah,*
> *Hilkhot Shabbat* 2:3

The observance of Kashrut is an example of an annoying series of mitzvot which I am glad not to have dropped because of some of the rather important surprises it has offered. Because it is a public observance, I have to justify it rather frequently, to my friends and certainly to myself. I find that whether I like it or not, Kashrut brings me into contact with a series of rather important questions: What is my responsibility to the calf that I eat . . .? Is the earth and the fullness thereof mine to do with as I will? What does it mean that a table should be an altar? Is eating indeed a devotional act? . . . If Kashrut makes me ask enough questions, often enough, I discover that its very provocative quality is one of its chief virtues for my religious life.

> Richard Israel in *The Condition of Jewish Belief*

23

WHY DO WE NEED ORGANIZED RELIGION?

We need organized religion for the same reason we need organized political parties or any organized social movement. In order to have any effect upon the world, people with similar aims, whether opposition to a war, the election of a particular candidate, or in the case of Judaism, the perfection of the world under the rule of God, must organize themselves.

Why then, if we recognize the need for organization in so many areas of social concern, does it seem illogical or undesirable to many people that there be organization in religion?

The answer lies in the understanding which most people have of religion, organized or not. They regard religion as an institution which regulates prayer and certain beliefs about God and whose relation to one's daily actions is tenuous at best. Consequently, many individuals feel that religion is or should be a "private affair," and that organized religion is unnecessary since private affairs need not be organized.

It may very well be that the religion to which many people have been exposed consists of little more than prayer and belief, and in such cases we would agree that organized religion is largely organized irrelevance. But as should be clear to anyone who knows the Jewish role in the world (see Question 5) this understanding of religion and organized religion has virtually nothing in common with Judaism. Judaism is concerned with organizing people to better the world. It is an all-encompassing value and action shaping way of life whose goals are the creation of moral

and holy* men and women, and ultimately a morally per-
fected world, and whose means are the system of Jewish
laws (Halakha).

A person who adopts this systematic way of life for himself alone would become a more moral and holy person, but
his impact upon the world would be minimal. Therefore, in
order to realize Judaism's goals of transforming the world,
all those individuals who are committed to these goals must
organize themselves. Some did about 3,500 years ago and
they are known as Jews. The Jews constitute, therefore,
the one people in the world whose basis of membership is a
shared ideal rather than a shared ethnicity, language or
land. Unlike all other nations wherein geography or ethnicity qualifies one for membership, all one must do in order to
become a Jew is to accept an ideal (Judaism) and its method
of implementation (Jewish laws). Thus, Judaism is not at all
an "organized religion" in the usual sense. The Jews are an
organized group of people of every racial and ethnic background who are committed to perfecting this world.

ISN'T IT ENOUGH TO BE AN ETHICAL
(OR MORAL) PERSON?

1. THE MEANING OF AN ETHICAL (OR MORAL)
PERSON
The meaning of the word ethical (or moral) as it is

---

*Holiness, kedusha in Hebrew, is a concept which originated with
Judaism and which is unique to religion. The secular individual cannot
possess the concepts of holiness and spirituality because these concepts
transcend the material world, the only reality which the non-believer
can recognize. Kedusha basically implies the elevation of the human
being from animal-like to God-like. It is one step higher than morality,
and can therefore be attained only if one is already moral. As Isaiah
declared: "God, the Holy One, is made holy through righteousness"
(Isaiah 5:16).

commonly used today is distorted. Often, after advocating the adoption of a religious-ethical system, we are challenged by questioners who claim to "know ethical people who do not believe in (and thus presumably do not need) a religious system." When asked to define an ethical person, these people generally answer "someone who doesn't hurt anybody." As this attitude is so prevalent, we are convinced that most people define an ethical person as one who does not hurt anyone. As widespread as this definition is, however, it is wrong. *A person whose ethical conduct consists of not hurting anyone is not ethical; such a person is merely not a criminal,* and not being a criminal does not mean that one is ethical. To be an ethical person involves the *active* pursuit of good.

Therefore, it is not "enough" to be ethical in the sense which most people understand this term. One must actively pursue right and good. To cite but a few examples: It is not enough to merely refrain from hurting other human beings; one must *intercede* on their behalf: "Do not stand by on the blood of your neighbor" (*Leviticus* 19:16).* Nor is it enough merely to refrain from personally performing an injustice, for in order to be ethical one must *seek out* and *rectify* injustices performed by others: "Justice, justice you shall pursue" (*Deuteronomy* 16:20); "And you shall burn the evil from out of your midst" (*Deuteronomy* 17:7 and elsewhere).

---

*The distinction between the morality which speaks of not hurting anyone, and Jewish morality which demands the positive helping of those who are in need, becomes clearer when one considers the case of Germany under the Nazis. According to the first definition of morality, the behavior of most Germans during the Holocaust was moral, since most Germans did not hurt anyone. However, when one considers moral obligations on the basis of Biblical demands such as "Do not stand by on the blood of your neighbor," one realizes that whereas such a German violated no secular or civil law, he had committed a serious crime under Jewish law.

The ideal which underlies the entire approach of Judaism to ethical behavior is the antithesis of the "let-everyone-do-his-own-thing" attitude. The ethical person must be "my brother's keeper." For example, "If your brother (any person who lives among you) becomes poor, then you shall sustain him, though he be a stranger or sojourner (a non-Jew) among you. And you shall not loan him money on interest, but you shall fear God." (*Leviticus* 25:35-6). In fact, *the entire Bible may be understood as a positive response to the question which Cain posed after murdering his brother Abel: "Am I my brother's keeper?"*

Precisely- because ethical behavior consists of positive acts, Judaism has developed what has come to be the most extensive system of ethical laws known to mankind (see, for example, the appendix). When one considers all these moral imperatives, it becomes clear that whether or not they care to admit it, most people are ethical only by the definition of "not hurting anybody," while they are ethically deficient by Judaism's definition of active involvement as "my brother's keeper." Be it helping Biafra, retarded children, Soviet Jewry and other Soviet dissidents, opposing totalitarianism, or supporting any other cause unrelated to their immediate lives, the majority of people are quite content to lead lives uncommitted to much else other than their own selves.

For this reason, the great majority of people are in deep need of an ethical system. Even the minority of people who do concern themselves with moral issues could use such a system. As Judaism long ago realized, and as twentieth-century man must realize now, *moral ideals do not suffice to create moral individuals and a moral world.* Judaism's ideals of universal peace and justice are by now virtually universally accepted ideals, and numerous ideologies (e.g., Christianity, Islam, Marxism and Communism, Humanism)* have arisen promising to realize these ideals without an ethical system such as Judaism's binding on their adherents. However, all the horrors perpetrated in the name of ideals constitute tragic but irrefutable testimony to the fact that idealism is not enough and that a detailed ethical system binding upon every individual is indispensable to achieving universal peace, justice and brotherhood. To achieve moral ends we need a moral system, and in the course of its 3500 year history Judaism has developed the most extensive (and in our view the most effective) ethical system known to mankind.

To be better at anything—from a sport to an art—a system is necessary. Why not a system for ethics?

2. ENOUGH FOR THE GENTILE; NOT ENOUGH FOR THE JEW

There are of course some individuals who are actively moral, and thus ethical by Judaism's definition. With regard to them, we would still commend the Jewish ethical system for even greater ethical proficiency, but Judaism would say that for the non-Jew this is "enough" while for the Jew it is not enough. In fact, for the non-Jew this is more than enough, for Judaism demands of the non-Jew only that he not lead an unethical life:** such a non-Jew

---

*For a Jewish assessment of some of these ideologies, see Question 4.

**Specifically, this means that non-Jews are held responsible for obeying what are known as "the seven laws of the children of Noah" (i.e., all mankind, as we are all descended from Noah). Since ancient times these laws have been understood as one positive law to establish a legal system and six prohibitions against idolatry, blasphemy, murder, sexual sins (incest, adultery and the like), theft, and eating from a living animal (see *Sanhedrin* 56a).

is entitled to "a portion in the world-to-come" (*Tosefta Sanhedrin* 13:2) and to material support whenever necessary from the Jewish community. He or she is in no way obligated to assume the burden of Judaism and its laws (though we would, be delighted if he or she would).

The Jew, however, is obligated to observe the Jewish laws so that the Jewish people may ultimately serve as a moral "light unto the nations" (*Isaiah* 49:6) and thereby influence the non-Jewish world to adopt the principles of ethical monotheism: one God and one moral standard. The Jew is obligated to do more than not lead an unethical life—he or she must lead an ethical life and a Jewish life. The Jew is required to participate in the historic attempt of Judaism to transform the world through personal implementation of Jewish law.

To summarize, Judaism with its systematic ethics is necessary because 1) most of us are not naturally moral; 2) those of us who do tend to moral sensitivity should be further sensitized to moral issues; and 3) it is not enough to *intend* to be a good person—one must have objective directives in order to translate good intentions into good actions. In the words of a prominent Canadian Reform Rabbi, Gunther Plaut: "One does not build character merely by desiring it; there must be habituation and this is achieved through *taryag mitzvot* (the 613 laws of the Torah)."

The taryag mitzvot *consist of "laws between man and man" (such as the laws of charity enumerated in the appendix) and those known as "laws between man and God" (such as observing the Sabbath and keeping kosher).*

Purposes of the Laws Between Man and God:

1. MORAL INDIVIDUALS
Through Self-Discipline

2. HOLINESS
Through Sanctification of Everyday Actions

3. A MORE MORAL WORLD
Through the Effects of the Laws

1. MORAL INDIVIDUALS
In order to lead an actively ethical life, a person must first train himself morally. It takes a great deal of practice to develop the strength of character needed to be an actively moral person and this can be done only by constantly exercising self-control. Thus, before it can help to achieve Judaism's goal of perfecting society, Halakha must first perfect the individual Jew. The Jew must train to become master over his impulses, and to prevent his impulses from becoming master over him. Only then will the individual be free, i.e., free to do what his mind (which should be guided by ethical principles) wants.

Admittedly, the notion of constant self-discipline leading to freedom is not easily accepted in a society which implores us to do whatever we, or more accurately, our impulses, desire. When society tells us to be free the implication is that self-discipline is inimical to such freedom. For freedom according to contemporary culture generally means doing whatever your physical impulses want.

But this is not freedom. *While the impulses may be liberated, the mind becomes enslaved.* The body demands comfort, and the mind becomes preoccupied with attaining pleasure; the body demands sex, and the mind becomes preoccupied with sex. To the extent to which the mind becomes preoccupied with the fulfillment of physical needs, the individual is not free.* Freedom means being able to say no to one's instincts when necessary (for ethical or other reasons). In every aspect of life self-discipline is the prerequisite of freedom. The physically free (i.e., free to do what is physically right) individual is the athlete or dancer who spends a lifetime disciplining his or her body. The artistically free (i.e., free to fulfill the demands of the art) individual is the virtuoso pianist who spent years training his or her fingers.

One purpose of Halakha is to render a person morally free (i.e., free to do what is morally right). Halakha is to ethics what Czerny exercises are to pianistic technique.**

2. HOLINESS

The second major purpose of Jewish law is the sanctifica-

---

*Once preoccupation with fulfilling physical desires starts, people often become incapable of resisting the demands of these desires, and an almost total abdication of the mind's freedom takes place. It is a basic tenet of the advertising industry, for example, that males can be manipulated through their sexual urge and advertisers consequently appeal far more often to men's sexual urges than to their minds.

**Halakhic self-discipline must not be equated with asceticism, however, since Halakha does not prohibit sensual or other forms of physical enjoyment. In fact, it commands us to partake of such joys, as they are viewed as gifts of God. For example: according to the Talmud, "In the future, a man will be required to give an accounting for every pleasurable food which he could have legitimately experienced, but which he refused to partake of" (*Jerusalem Talmud*, end of *Tractate Kiddushin*). Similarly, it is a *mitzvah* to fulfill the sexual needs of both partners in a marriage. What Halakha does prohibit is becoming preoccupied with, and enslaved to, the need for physical pleasure. Thus, one might say that in Halakha all needs may be satisfied, but not at all times, and only up to a given point.

tion and ethical elevation of man by bringing God as well as moral concerns into our everyday actions. In compelling us to devote a full seventh of our lives to the observance of the Shabbat, or to recite a blessing to God before and after eating, or through the law that instructs us when shopping not to inquire of a storekeeper the price of an item which we do not intend to buy (*Mishnah Bava Meziah* 4:10), Halakha constantly reminds us of our obligations and potential as men and women created in the image of God.

The Jew who observes the cycle of Jewish life is given the opportunity to sanctify his or her life in a manner that simply cannot be done in secular society. Compare, for example, the Jewish observance of its New Year (Rosh Ha-Shanah), with the secular celebration of January 1. In Judaism Rosh Ha-Shanah inaugurates ten days of ethical and spiritual soul-searching leading up to Yom Kippur—the Day of Atonement. The meaning of Rosh Ha-Shanah should be contrasted with the meaninglessness of New Year's. Whereas the latter exists for party-going and merriment, the Jewish New Year, though of course a celebration, is primarily a serious day of introspection. Moreover the Jewish New Year's difference is apparent throughout the holiday, and not only when Jews are at synagogue. A significant part of this difference can be attributed to the Jewish law which forbids the handling of money on holy days. If the handling of money were forbidden on New Year's, it would never again be celebrated. The same comparison can be made regarding the observance of Rosh Ha-Shanah between religious and secular Jews in Israel. To secular Israelis Rosh Ha-Shanah is merely a Hebrew January 1: a national holiday for travel, parties and fun.

Halakha gives us the possibility of bringing an aspect of holiness to the seemingly trivial events of our lives; or more poetically, in the words of Abraham J. Heschel, "It gives us the opportunity to perceive the infinite even as we are performing the finite." A couple moves into a home and there is a religious ceremony in which they hammer a *mezuzah** onto their doorpost. Every time they enter the home the *mezuzah* (which is traditionally kissed on the way in and on the way out) is there to remind them of their obligations in the home in which they live. When they leave the house it is there to remind them of their obligations in the world into which they are going. What emerges from observance of Halakha is a sense that there is nothing in life which is inherently petty but that all the acts of one's life can be holy.** This notion in turn suggests a corollary belief. If your actions are not petty but geared towards fulfilling a higher ideal, then you, as the performer of these acts, are not a petty person.

---

*The *mezuzah* (doorpost) is the distinctive mark of the Jewish home. It consists of a small roll of parchment on which is written the *shema* (the Jewish prayer affirming the unity of God) and two Biblical passages concerning the love of God and His precepts (*Deuteronomy* 6:4-9; 11:13-21). The *mezuzah* is enclosed in a metal or wooden case, with the word *Shadai* (Almighty) written on the back of the parchment and made visible through a small opening near the top of the case. According to Maimonides, the purpose of the *mezuzah* is to make us constantly aware of the Divine oneness and of our moral duties (*Yad Hazakah, Hilkhot Mezuzah* 5:5).

**There is no area of life which Jewish practice cannot elevate and make holy, for Judaism considers nothing natural to be holy or profane in and of itself. Unlike classical Christianity, for example, which demeaned the sexual act and forbade its holy men and women to engage in it, Judaism viewed sexual relations as one more way to achieve holiness. As Nachmanides, a central medieval Jewish commentator and philosopher, wrote: "The act of sexual union is holy and pure . . . The Lord created all things in accordance with His wisdom and whatever He created cannot possibly be shameful or ugly . . . When a man is in union with his wife in a spirit of holiness or purity, the Divine presence is with them" (*Iggeret ha-Kodesh* 13c).

3. A MORE MORAL WORLD

Do Shabbat and Kashrut make me or the world more moral?

Many people consider the Jewish laws between man and God to be either meaningless rituals performed by the believer in order to please God or as religiously or emotionally symbolic but ethically irrelevant gestures.* Consequently, basic Jewish laws such as Shabbat (on which day, among other actions, it is forbidden to make a fire, watch television, or work) and Kashrut (which prohibits the eating of some animals and regulates the manner in which permitted animals are to be slaughtered) are deemed irrelevant and/or irrational and therefore of little or no significance to modern man. Because this opinion is so common, it is necessary to state at the outset that *the laws between man and God are both ethically relevant and rational.*

---

*Unfortunately, this tendency to deny a rational and/or ethical meaning to Jewish laws between man and God is common today among Jews in both the conservative and liberal camps. On the one hand some very observant Jews preach the necessity of blind observance without the attempt to penetrate to the laws' relevance, and these people view negatively any attempt to provide rational explanations for Jewish laws, fearing that such explanations will make these laws seem human rather than divine in origin. On the other hand, some liberal Jews are content to define the laws between man and God as rituals devoid of rational and/or ethical purpose, and consequently dismiss observance of these laws as irrelevant. Thus, though they proceed from opposite viewpoints, neither of these types of Jews can communicate the rational and ethical significance of that aspect of Judaism which renders it unique— Jewish law. This unwillingness to seek out the meaning and purpose of Jewish laws was denounced in the strongest possible terms 800 years ago by Moses Maimonides, when he wrote in the *Guide To The Perplexed* (Part 3 Chapter 31): "There is a group of human beings who

The Torah itself (the source of all these supposedly meaningless, or at best, outdated fiats) asserts that its laws can
and should be understood as rational laws dedicated to the
achievement of its moral goals. The book of *Deuteronomy*
(4:6) makes this point when it instructs the Jews to obey
Jewish laws in these words: "Observe and do them; for (the
laws) will render you wise and profound in the eyes of other
nations, and when they hear all these statutes, they shall
say 'Surely this great nation is a wise and profound
people'." The Torah's point here is obvious. Only people
observing wise and profound laws can be expected to be
viewed by outsiders as a "wise and profound people." A
people observing irrational rituals could hardly be expected
to serve as an ethical model to rational outsiders.

---

consider it a grievous thing that causes should be given for any law; what
would please them most is that the intellect would not find a meaning for
the commandments and prohibitions. What compels them to feel thus is a
sickness that they find in their souls, a sickness to which they are unable
to give utterance and of which they cannot furnish a satisfactory account. For they think that if those laws were useful in this existence and
had been given to us for this or that reason, it would be as if they derived
from the reflection and understanding of some intelligent being. If, however, there is a thing for which the intellect could not find any meaning
at all and that does not lead to something useful, it indubitably derives
from God: for the reflection of man would lead to no such thing" (S.
Pines' translation of the *Guide*, Chicago: 1963, pp. 523-4). Following in
the Maimonidean tradition, the contemporary Anglo-Jewish scholar
Louis Jacobs has written, ". . . nowhere in the whole of the biblical
record is there the faintest suggestion that God imposes upon man arbi-
trary rules which must be observed purely on the grounds that God so
desires" (see Jacobs' essay "The Relationship Between Religion and
Ethics in Jewish Thought" in *Religion and Morality*, edited by Gene
Outka and John P. Reeder Jr., New York: 1973, p. 156).

Shabbat

Let us analyze, for example, a Jewish institution suffering widespread neglect in today's world—the Shabbat.*
Most Jews (including those far removed from observance of
Jewish law) acknowledge that the Jewish Sabbath was the
model for Western and Islamic man's weekly day of rest.
Unfortunately, however, their appreciation of the Shabbat
begins and ends with this insight. For while they proudly
note that a weekly day of rest has become more or less
universally observed, they are utterly ignorant of the
meaning of the Shabbat, though this ignorance does not
inhibit them from maintaining that observance of Shabbat
laws is unnecessary.

Yet those fortunate enough to have experienced authentic Shabbatot recognize that from the observance of the
Shabbat flow the deepest and most influential insights into
the human condition, and benefits of the highest moral and
spiritual sort. Before analyzing these insights and benefits,
however, let us note two reasons why even the one generally acknowledged purpose of the Shabbat, to provide us
with rest, distorts the Shabbat's true purpose. First, it
implies that the Shabbat is basically an act of social
hygiene, a health measure; and second, it implies that the
Shabbat was created for the sake of the rest of the week.

The first implication is a distortion because the benefits
accruing to the well-being of our bodies through Shabbat
observance are greatly superseded by the intended bene-

---

*The Shabbat is a particularly significant example because occurring
fifty-two times a year it occupies a central role in Jewish life. *The Shabbat in Jewish law is of equal (if not greater) significance to Yom Kippur*,
the Day of Atonement. It is probably unique among all the religions of
the world that a holiday falling fifty-two times a year is the most important day of the year for its people.

fits to the well-being of our minds and souls. The second notion is completely in error. The Shabbat was not created for the sake of the rest of the week; rather the Shabbat was created to be the focal point of the preceding six days of the week. To cite two examples: Jewish law directs us to save our best food and clothing for the Shabbat, and there are no names in Hebrew for the weekdays, as they are all enumerated in reference to their proximity to the Shabbat. At the conclusion of the daily morning prayers, the Jew identifies the days of the week as: "Today is the first (second, third etc.) day of the week counting towards the Shabbat."

What then is the goal of Shabbat, if not to have us rest?

Shabbat Goal: *A taste of the Messianic Age by creating a day of peace on earth through observance of the Shabbat laws.*

I   Peace Between Man and Himself
II   Peace Between Man and His Fellow Man
III   Peace Between Man and Nature
IV   Peace Between Man and God

I Peace Between Man and Himself

On the Shabbat man should return to his own mind and body, and for this purpose the Shabbat laws are designed to produce a state of inner peace. To achieve this state, *the laws' intent is to inhibit use of external sources of energy; and its prohibitions include, therefore, travel, radio, television, telephone and other use of machinery.*

By not driving, watching television, using machinery, or otherwise relying on external sources of creativity, people are compelled to return to themselves for creativity. All creativity on the Shabbat should come from within the human being. Thus, for example, one can sing but not play instruments or records; or one can read, but not write. Writing is forbidden because of its inherent reliance upon an external source of creativity, a pen or pencil. When writing, one relies upon the writing implement to create new words, but when reading, all creativity is within a person (his mind) since the words have already been created.

All week we rely upon, and often become enslaved to, external sources of creativity, amusement, etc., especially in the form of technology. On the Shabbat, however, man is freed from enslavement to technology. While most modern men and women cannot conceive of life without cars, television, or telephones, one who observes the Shabbat conceives of life in these terms. How can he not, considering that the Shabbat observer spends one-seventh of his life (ten full years if he lives to be seventy) without relying on any of these things?*

The Shabbat also compels the individual to reflect on the most significant question concerning himself and technology. After spending six days at work, creating, utilizing and expanding technology, the individual is forced on the seventh day to reflect on the question: *work and technology towards what purpose? for what end?*

---

*Perhaps this idea will strike some as more palatable when put not in the words of the Torah, but in the words of a contemporary and untraditional figure: Norman Mailer. During Mr. Mailer's campaign for mayor of New York in 1969, he suggested a radically new idea: Super-Sunday. On this day, Mailer suggested, traffic and transport should be minimized in the city, radio and TV would limit broadcasting, and peace would reign in New York. Many found this idea to be another brilliant spin-off from a brilliant mind. Traditional Jews know, however, that Super-Saturdays have been observed in their communities for over three thousand years.

II Peace Between Man and His Fellow Man

BETWEEN MAN AND HIS FAMILY

By insuring that we refrain from reliance upon the in-animate, Shabbat laws compel us to seek relationships with the animate: first, ourselves, and then our family and neighbors. Certainly, we who have experienced the Shab-bat can testify to one nearly universal consequence of Shabbat observance: the strengthening of family unity and harmony.

The withdrawal from technology not only forces a person to think and introspect, but to do so within the confines of his family and friends (because of the prohibition of travel on the Shabbat). This is particularly significant in the United States, for Americans tend to associate free time and recreation with leaving one's usual surroundings. Pleasure and meaning during weekends are sought as far away from one's home as time and money permit.

The Jewish notion of how to utilize free time is significantly different. Judaism wishes that a person endow the place where he or she spends Shabbat, usually the home, with a measure of spirituality that does not exist there during the week. In this way, the family and home are elevated at all times on Shabbat. The meals are a particularly fine example. The Friday night meal in a traditional Jewish home is a lengthy one in which all members of the family participate in beautiful singing and in much talk. Both of us can testify that in our homes the Talmudic injunction forbidding one to eat with others without discussing Torah (Torah defined here in the broadest sense, as moral concerns) was carried out every Friday night. Talks would range over politics, Israel, family news, foreign affairs, American Jewry, and, of course, Jewish sources such as the weekly portion of the Torah reading. Often, discussions would go on for hours, because *unlike the rest*

*of the week no one had another appointment to run to at the
end of the meal.* If such talk had been stopped to watch a
basketball game, or to go to a movie, this would have indicated that basketball and movies are more significant
than values, family discussion, and Judaism.

When we speak about the effects of the lengthy Friday
night meal on the family, we often encounter reactions of
envy, and a feeling that in their families (the listeners') it
would not work. They question whether their family would
find enough to talk about for two or three hours, a question
which is unfortunately a valid one for most American Jews
and non-Jews. A common symptom of the contemporary
breakdown of family life is the inability of members to
communicate with one another on matters of any importance.* The Shabbat serves, therefore, not only as a
day of reunion and elevation for the family, but also as a
day which challenges a family to confront a question which
many families prefer to avoid: can the family members
communicate with one another?

The provoking of a situation wherein all members of the
family are compelled to talk to each other is one more way
in which the Shabbat fosters family unity. Parents and
children begin to relate, and as regards the husband-wife
relationship, the case can be stated succinctly: in households where the Shabbat is observed there are no golf or
football widows.

BETWEEN MAN AND HIS FELLOW MAN

In order to achieve the Shabbat goal of peace between
man and man, the Shabbat laws actually realize the funda-

---

*One study done two years ago, for example, found that in the aver-
age home the husband and wife spend only 27½ minutes per week in
discussion of issues, that is issues unrelated to immediate family problems such as who needs the car or who will pick up the groceries.

mental Jewish belief in the equality of all human beings.*
Exodus 20:10 instructs us: "The Seventh day is a Shabbat
unto the Lord your God, on it you shall not do any manner
of work, neither you, nor your son, nor your daughter, nor
your man-servant, nor your maid-servant, nor your cattle,
nor the stranger that is within your gate." We are all serv-
ants of God and one servant cannot assert mastery over
another. Though in the current world such an ideal may not
yet be economically or socially functional in daily life, on at
least one day a week (a day that is considered to be a
"foretaste of the world to come") the Jew must put this
ideal into practice in the hope that it will influence his behavior and that of those around him all week long. Thus,
while Utopians of the Right and Left preach revolution to
achieve their dreams of a world in which no man may dominate another, Jewish law has rendered this the Jews' *reality* at least one day every week throughout Jewish history.

---

*In addition to the laws of Shabbat, the equality of men is legislated
in the Bible three times (*Exodus* 12:49, *Leviticus* 24:22, *Numbers* 15:16):
"There shall be but one manner of law for the native (Jew) and for the
stranger who lives among you." And the Talmud notes (*Mishnah
Sanhedrin* 4:5): ". . . therefore was Adam created singly . . . for the
sake of peace between men, that one man shall not say to another: 'my
father was greater than yours'." The same Mishnah also informs us that
Adam was created singly "in order to teach us that he who destroys one
person it is as if he destroyed the entire world, and likewise he who
saves one person it is as if he saved the entire world." (It may be noted
that though some Jewish scholars read the above text as "he who destroys one *Jewish* person," this is an obvious perversion of the text, as
the proof for the statement derives from Adam, and Adam of course was
not a Jew.) One of the most far-reaching assertions of the equality of all
men in the eyes of God is the statement in the medieval *Tanna de Be
Eliyahu* (M. Friedman edition, Vienna: 1902, p. 48): ". . . I call heaven
and earth to witness that whether it be Gentile or Israelite, man or
woman, slave or handmaid, according to the deeds which he does, so will
the Holy Spirit rest on him."

III Peace Between Man and Nature

On the Shabbat man should return to nature and not interfere with it. To achieve this peaceful state with nature, the Shabbat laws' intent is to inhibit tampering with nature; hence, *both creation and destruction are prohibited on the Shabbat.* As examples, one should not start a fire (therefore no smoking or cooking on Shabbat) or extinguish a fire which already exists; nor plant a tree (creation) or tear a leaf from a tree (destruction).

For one day each week specific Shabbat laws insure that we do not rule over nature, just as other laws insure that on this day we do not rule over fellow human beings or animals.

IV Peace Between Man and God

All week we devote ourselves to ourselves but "Shabbat," the Torah tells us, "is to God." All week we concern ourselves with what we want, but on Shabbat we reflect on what God wants of us. Shabbat is God's day. This is the ultimate Shabbat goal because it can be attained only once we have begun to realize peace between ourselves and our fellow human beings, peace between ourselves and nature, and peace within ourselves. Only when we have started to achieve peace with this world are we free to transcend ourselves and approach God. This is accomplished in at least three ways:
1. Prayer and meditation.
2. Study of Torah.
3. Sanctification of the day.

1. PRAYER AND MEDITATION
Rabbi Samson Raphael Hirsch, the father of Neo-Ortho-

doxy, noted that the Hebrew verb to pray is reflexive (*l'hitpallel*) and means to "judge oneself." Jewish prayer is therefore a form of personal self-judgment, and because most prayers in the *siddur* (prayer book) are collectively oriented, it also stimulates communal meditation and self-judgement. A Jew approaches God in a personal quest for ethical excellence: "O my God! guard my tongue from evil and my lips from speaking falsely . . . Open my heart to the Torah, and let my soul pursue your commandments . . . Let the words of my mouth and the meditation of my heart be acceptable before you . . ." (from the end prayer of the Amidah). Likewise during the solemn *Kedushah* the whole community of Israel accepts upon itself the Jewish role: "We will sanctify Your name in this world [through our actions] as God's name is already sanctified in the heavens."

Unfortunately, the modern synagogue has lost much of its earlier majestic simplicity—in Hebrew it is called simply a "meeting place"—and has become for many Jews a colder and more formal entity than it should be. But a beautiful Shabbat service is an emotional experience which can leave its participants moved morally, spiritually, and emotionally as no symphony or play can.

2. STUDY OF TORAH

The study of Torah is the most direct manner in which man can meet God, since each new insight and thought is a form of new revelation. (The intellectual and ethical challenges of one small Torah portion are discussed on p. 158ff.) For the person who studies Torah, God can never be an abstract and unapproachable Deity.

3. SANCTIFICATION OF THE DAY

Life is composed of the material and the spiritual. During the week the material tends to dominate. But Shabbat is a day on which matter is relegated to the background and the spiritual brought to the foreground. During the Shabbat, 25 hours in which time, not space, is sanctified (to borrow an idea from A.J. Heschel), man is given an opportunity to relate to the One Who has no body and is composed of no matter.

Let us conclude this discussion of Shabbat with an analysis of the variant wordings of the Shabbat commandment in the two versions of the Ten Commandments. *Exodus* 20:8 reads *"Remember* the Shabbat day to make it holy" while *Deuteronomy* 5:12 instructs us to *"Observe* the Shabbat day to make it holy." What does this single difference in wording mean? One refers to ends, the other to means. We must "Remember" the ideals of Shabbat and we must "Observe" the specific Shabbat laws without which the ideals remain abstract. By this significant choosing of words, the Torah also warns us against tendencies which we often encounter in the Jewish community. On the one hand, there are Jews who are so preoccupied with every aspect of the "Observe" that they forget to "Remember" the accompanying ideals which the Shabbat laws are meant to implant. We have met children from such homes who laugh when we speak to them of the ideals of Shabbat. For them Shabbat was more a day of terror when they were apt to be punished for actions which their parents viewed as violations of the "Observe" of the Shabbat. On the other hand are Jews, far more numerous than those in the first category, who claim that they need obey only the "Remember." These Jews think that they can realize the ideals of Shabbat (and Judaism generally) without observing the laws which render these ideals real and tangible.

The Torah therefore warns us against both tendencies by instructing us to both *Zachor* (Remember) the Shabbat day to make it holy, and to *Shamor* (Observe) the laws so that we can remember the ideals.

Kashrut

While Shabbat practice is usually ignored but seldom disparaged by modern Jews, we wish to focus attention now on a practice that is often ignored and disparaged—Kashrut (keeping kosher). Ask most Jews why the laws of Kashrut exist, and you are likely to receive this authoritative reply: "It was a health measure. For example, pigs were forbidden to Jews so that Jews would not get trichinosis. But with modern health codes we certainly don't need such measures today."*

Unfortunately, this common opinion is an example of the "law of ignorant opinions authoritatively stated" which posits that in politics and religion the less a person knows the more authoritatively he speaks. Worse yet, this view of Kashrut is reflective of a greater error regarding Jewish law. It seems that many Jews are convinced that Jewish law does not constitute an ethical code but is really a health code. They reason that Kashrut was instituted to prevent disease, the Shabbat to prevent heart attacks due to overwork, circumcision to prevent cervical cancer, and so forth.

The facts, however, are completely different. Kashrut,

---

*The assumption that Kashrut is a health measure raises an interesting question. How do the people who believe that the prohibition of eating pigs saved Jews from death by trichinosis account for the Jews anticipating the negative effects of eating pig thousands of years before physicians knew about it? They must concede that either the Bible was written by God or by veritable supermen who made medical discoveries thousands of years before anyone else. In either case, persons holding such beliefs should adopt a more respectful attitude towards the laws of Kashrut, insofar as they might be based on other medical knowledge that the modern world does not yet know. We, of course, do not look to Kashrut as a source of medical benefits but as laws leading to moral sensitivity and holiness.

like all Jewish laws, is saturated with moral meaning. The
four major ethical purposes of Kashrut fall into two categories.* With regard to the Jews Kashrut aims

1. to cause revulsion at bloodshed;
2. to instill self-discipline.

With regard to the animals Kashrut aims

1. to limit the number of edible animals, thus serving as
a compromise with Judaism's ideal of vegetarianism;
2. to render the slaughter of edible animals as painless
as possible.

The growth of the ideal of Kashrut is evident in the
Torah. Ideally, according to Judaism, we should be vegeta-
rians.** In the Garden of Eden, a Biblical representation of
Utopia, man was not to kill any animal but was to eat only
of the Garden's fruits and vegetables (*Genesis* 1:27-9).
After leaving Utopia, however, primitive man hunted and
did so without consideration for the animals' suffering.
Consequently, both for the animals' sake and for the sake of
mankind's ethical development, laws were soon enacted to
regulate the eating of animals. First, men were forbidden
to eat the limb of a living animal, an ordinance so old and
universal that it is one of the seven laws which Judaism

---

*It must be recognized that in citing the ethical component in the
laws of Kashrut, we are not imposing our own views. The Torah itself
explicitly relates Kashrut to higher ideals: "And you shall be men of a
holy calling unto Me, and you shall not eat any meat that is torn *(trefah)*
in the field" (*Exodus* 22:30); ". . . for you are a holy people unto the Lord
your God. You shall not seethe a kid in its mother's milk" (*Deuteronomy*
14:21). *Leviticus* 11:44-5 similarly stresses the theme of holiness in the
laws of Kashrut.

**Thus, in the book of *Isaiah* (11:6, 7, 9), when he depicts the Mes-
sianic days the Prophet automatically presupposes that creatures will be
herbivorous.

obligates all people to observe. Next, the Torah forbade
the eating of an animal's blood "because the life (or alter-
nately soul) of a living creature is in its blood" (See
Leviticus 3:17; 7:26; 17:10-4; *Deuteronomy* 12:15-6; and
12:23-25). The purpose of this ancient law was to induce
revulsion at bloodshed, and it seems that there is indeed a
direct correlation between the Torah's prohibition of eating
blood and the extremely low incidence of homicide among
Jews. As Professor Jacob Milgrom of the University of
California at Berkeley has noted: "This prohibition is not
found anywhere else in the ancient Near East . . . That
none of Israel's neighbors possess this absolute and universal binding prohibition means that it cannot be a vestige
of a primitive taboo, but the result of a deliberate reasoned
enactment. This is clear from the *rationale appended to the
law: blood is life*" (emphasis ours) (*Leviticus* 17:11, 14;
Deuteronomy 12:23; Milgrom's observation appears in the
Encyclopedia Judaica 4:1115).

Later, in order to prevent the Jew from going out and
killing any animal he saw, the Torah, realistically com-
promising with its vegetarian ideal (perhaps one reason for
the compromise was that nutritional knowledge did not
suffice to enable people to subsist solely on a vegetarian
diet), divided the animal kingdom into permitted (kosher)
and non-permitted halves. At the same time, Judaism instituted its laws of slaughter, the primary aim of which was
to reduce the suffering of the slaughtered animals as much
as possible. To cite a few of many possible examples, a
wounded animal was declared non-kosher to insure that
animals be killed as quickly and painlessly as possible *with
one cut;* the *shochet* (slaughterer) could not be just any
Jew—he had to be particularly pious and educated (since
such a person would presumably be most careful to mini-
mize the animal's suffering); and an animal slaughtered

with a dull, blunted knife is not kosher. One particularly
poignant example of Judaism's humaneness and of Kashrut's aim to morally sensitize the human being, is the
Torah's prohibition against slaughtering an animal and its
offspring on the same day (*Leviticus* 22:28).

Thus the laws which put half of the animal world off
limits to Jewish tables in conjunction with the myriad laws
insuring humane slaughter of the permitted half make up
the systematic ethics of Judaism with regard to food.*

But this is not all. Kashrut, like all Jewish laws, also
serves the crucial purpose of strengthening each Jew's
self-control. In a famous passage in *Midrash Tanhuma
Shmini* 7 (written about 1,500 years ago) Rav states that
"the Mitzvot (commandments; in this instance Kashrut)
were given solely in order to train people. For what does it
matter to the Blessed Holy One . . . about the "purity" or
"impurity" of the animals we eat? It is clear, then, that the
mitzvot were given solely for the purpose of training
people."

---

*Kashrut may be regarded as but one part of Judaism's systematic
ethics concerning the treatment of animals. Under the heading *tzaar
ba'alei chayyim* (prevention of cruelty to animals) the Torah legislated
over 3,000 years ago that 1) just as you rest on the Shabbat, so must
your animal rest (*Exodus* 20:10); 2) "You shall not plow with an ox and
mule harnessed together" (*Deuteronomy* 22:10), since being of unequal
size and strength both animals would suffer; 3) if a man comes across a
nest of birds, he cannot slaughter the mother bird with the young, but
must send the mother bird away to spare her feelings (*Deuteronomy*
22:6), for as Maimonides has written, "The pain of the animals under
such circumstances is very great" (*Guide To The Perplexed* 3:48);
4) while treading out the corn, the ox (or any other animal) cannot be
muzzled (*Deuteronomy* 25:4) so that while working in the field the animal
will be free to eat as much as it desires. Later in the Talmudic period,
the rabbis legislated that it is forbidden for one to eat in the morning
before he has fed his animals (*Talmud Berakhot* 40a) or to purchase an
animal if he is not sure that he can provide sufficient food for it.

The question is often posed: Is Kashrut really related to ethics or holiness—after all, it's not what goes into a man's mouth but what comes out that makes him impure (echoing Jesus in *Mark* 7:19)?

We would answer: *Every time a Jew sits down to eat a kosher meal he or she is reminded that the animal being eaten is a creature of God, that the death of such a creature cannot be taken lightly, that hunting for sport is forbidden, that we cannot treat any living thing irresponsibly, and that we are responsible for what happens to other beings (human and animal) even if we did not come into contact with them.* Therefore, as an example of the latter concern, a Boston rabbinic court declared grapes picked by oppressed Chicano workers non-kosher; and perhaps we may similarly declare the skins of baby seals which were clubbed to death non-kosher to be worn.

Three times a day, Richard Israel has noted, "a Jew must ask himself certain questions before he can eat. Was this animal killed in a cruel manner? Was all the blood extracted? Is the earth and the fullness thereof mine to do with as I will? What does it mean that the table should be an altar?"

Some might dismiss this Jewish concern with diet as pettiness, feeling that religion should deal only with exalted things. But Judaism holds that *there is no area of life that is not capable of becoming exalted.* Eating is petty only when the people who are eating are petty. In the Jewish home where Kashrut is observed, where people make a blessing to God before eating, and where the Jewish injunction to speak of matters of Torah during the meal is maintained, eating is not petty. It is one more act in the attempt by man to make all of life holy. As Samuel Dresner has written, "In eating a slice of bread, we can discover God, in drinking a cup of wine, we can sanctify the Sabbath, *in preparing a piece of meat we can learn something* *of the reverence of life." (The Jewish Dietary Laws, New York: 1966, p. 41, emphasis ours).* *

----

*Aside from the important moral and social ideals communicated by the laws of Kashrut, there is yet one more effect which must be noted— the relationship of Kashrut to the social cohesion of the Jewish community. When a non-observant Jew or non-Jew travels to a city where he has no acquaintances, he often remains there without ever coming to know the inhabitants. But when we travel, our observance of Kashrut immediately insures that we meet local people. Usually we call the rabbi to inquire where kosher food can be obtained and more often than not an inquiry of this sort results in a dinner invitation, either to the house of the rabbi or to the home of a layman he might suggest. This has been our experience throughout the United States and on five continents. Later we go to synagogue where we meet other Jews, and befriend new people. Because we share a value-system and a life-style there is at least some instantaneous rapport between us. When Kashrut is observed, no Jew is ever alone in a city where there are other Jews.

Question 3

IF JUDAISM IS SUPPOSED TO MAKE
PEOPLE BETTER, HOW DO YOU ACCOUNT
FOR UNETHICAL RELIGIOUS JEWS?

HOW DO YOU ACCOUNT FOR ETHICAL
PEOPLE WHO ARE NOT RELIGIOUS?

*The Torah is to the soul of man what rain is to the soil; rain
makes any seed put into the soil grow, producing nourish-
ing as well as poisonous plants. The Torah also helps him
who is striving for self-perfection, while it increases the
impurity of heart of those that remain uncultivated.*
> Elijah, the Gaon of Vilna, in his commentary
> on *Proverbs* 24:31 and 25:4.

*. . . how is one to account for the goodness of so many
irreligionists? Very simply. Men often behave better than
their philosophies. They cannot be expected to persist in
doing so. In the end, how a man thinks must affect how he
acts: atheism must finally, if not in one generation, then in
several, remake the conduct of atheists in the light of its
own logic.*
> Milton Steinberg, *Anatomy of Faith*

A problem which disturbs every sensitive Jew is the existence of Jews who observe many Jewish laws but who are, nevertheless, immoral people. This is a crucial problem because it is the existence of such people which often serves to invalidate religion in the eyes of others, and to make it easy to dismiss religion as either mechanical gestures or hypocrisy.

I

Observance of Jewish laws which are characterized as between man and God (e.g., Kashrut, prayer, certain Shabbat laws) **do not render one more moral unless these laws are observed with the intention of becoming more moral through their observance.** * To expect otherwise, to expect that mechanical observance of Jewish religious law will automatically create morally superior individuals, is to confer upon Jewish law some magical quality which one would deem absurd if applied to any other area of life. Can one be expected to grasp the meaning of Shakespeare by mechanically reading his words without the intention of learning something from his works? Is it not possible to read Shakespeare's plays and to get little or nothing out of them? Is Shakespeare then to be considered worthless?

This relationship between observance and moral intent is hardly some "modern" interpretation of the way in which Jewish law functions. Judaism has always recognized that observance of man-God laws can have but a minimal moral effect upon an individual when he or she observes them

---

*For a discussion of the moral ideals which Jewish laws try to promote see Question 2.

without the intention of becoming a more moral person through them. The Prophets vehemently attacked those Jews whose mechanical observance of these laws betrayed a lack of concern for the ethical principles underlying them (see, for example, *Jeremiah* 7).

This point was also forcefully developed in the thirteenth century by Nachmanides, one of the great standard Rabbinic commentators on the Torah, in his commentary on *Leviticus* 19:2, "You shall be holy because I the Lord God am holy." This general injunction to "be holy," the commentator pointed out, seems to be somewhat out of character with the rest of the 613 commandments, for the Torah generally gives specific commandments rather than such general rules. Nachmanides here offers a subtle yet powerful insight. He notes that though the Torah forbids many things in its laws, merely avoiding the forbidden would not in and of itself create a good human being. He cites as an example the fact that the Torah permits, even advocates, eating *well* (referring to *Deuteronomy* 8:10), but the Torah does not specifically outlaw gluttony. Therefore, Nachmanides declares in a startling phrase, it is conceivable that a man "could be repugnant with the permission of the Torah!" Without actually violating a specific Torah law, one could lead a rather repulsive life (as one could, for example, be a repulsive driver without actually violating any traffic laws). It is for this reason, says Nachmanides, that the Torah issued the injunction to "be holy"—to guard against those who observe the letter of the law while making a mockery of its intent. Thus, to repeat, it is not enough to obey Jewish religious law; one must do so with the intention of achieving the moral excellence which Jewish law is designed to effect.

Unfortunately, in the course of the last few hundred years, with all their cataclysmic developments in Jewish life, certain extremes have developed within Judaism which have had negative impacts on Jewish life. Most important, the essential balance within Judaism of means and ends has been upset. Significant elements on Judaism's liberal left, for example, have emphasized only the Jewish ends of brotherhood and justice, while ignoring, if not outright opposing, the Jewish means to these ends, Jewish law. Often these people so preoccupied themselves with universal goals that they ceased being Jews; and it is doubtful whether those who dropped the means perpetuated Judaism's moral ends.

On the other hand, significant elements on the fundamentalist right (often in reaction to the leftist reformers' denial of Jewish law) came to emphasize only the Jewish means, the laws, while ignoring the universal and moral goals for whose realization the Jewish laws exist. These people came to care more about laws than about people.

The Jew who observes Jewish man-God laws while behaving in a loathsome manner towards his fellow man or woman is treating these laws as exercises in ritual rather than as moral training. The result is observance which is morally, hence religiously, worthless.

II

The premise of the original question is in error, for **a Jew is not religious if he observes Jewish laws between man and God, but not between man and man.** To anyone at all familiar with Judaism this statement is as obviously true as the statement that a citizen of the United States is not considered law-abiding if he violates half of the American legal code. We feel compelled to state this, however, because of the unfortunate fact that religion is so often associated in people's minds solely with acts between man and God.

Such acts, however, are but one part of Judaism (and

even these have profound ethical implications). Vast quantities of Jewish law and religious literature are concerned solely with actions between one individual and another, and these laws are Halakhically as binding as Kashrut, Tefillin and prayer. There are general ethical rules such as "Love your neighbor as yourself" (*Leviticus* 19:18), and there are innumerable specific and subtle ethical laws, as for example, the previously cited law which forbids a Jew to inquire of a storekeeper the price of an item, if he has no real interest in buying it (*Mishnah Bava Metziah* 4:10).

Judaism is so concerned with knowledge of and precision in ethics that it declares that "an ignoramus (i.e., one ignorant of the laws) cannot be a pious person" (*Mishnah Avot* 2:5). Thus, to call a person who is observant of man-God laws but negligent in his observance of the ethical laws an observant or religious Jew is a contradiction in terms, for he is violating vast portions of Jewish law. The highest religious appellation in Judaism is *hasid*, which means one who practices righteous and kindly deeds.

The following ethical laws are taken from nine verses (10-18) in *Leviticus* 19. *Is a Jew who violates these Torah laws religious or observant?*

Laws:

1) to give charity to the poor and to the stranger;
2) not to cheat or mislead people;
3) not to oppress a worker by not paying him promptly;
4) for a judge, not to favor either the rich (out of respect) or the poor (out of sympathy), and to thus always dispense justice;
5) not to gossip;
6) not to stand by while another's blood is being shed;
7) not to take revenge or even to bear a grudge;
8) to show love to one's neighbor as to oneself.

It should be clear from the above that an unethical Jew is

neither observant nor religious. Thus, we fervently hope
that Jews who observe some of Judaism's laws while remaining unethical, will either:

a) come to understand that the Prophet's words "Why
do I (God) need your sacrifices" (*Isaiah* 1:11) were meant
quite literally, since God has no "personal" need for their
selective ritualistic observances, and consequently they
will make a moral improvement; or

b) stop putting on the pretense of being observant, religious Jews, for through this they cause a most abhorrent
religious sin, *hillul Hashem*, the profanation of God's
name;* and consequently they will become as neglectful of
the laws between man and God as they are of those between man and man.

III

Before proceeding to a discussion of the reasons for the
existence of ethical people who are not religious, we wish to
note three significant points relating to observant Jews and
their behavior.

1. Violent crime is virtually unkown among observant
Jews and this is as true in societies where Jews constitute
the majority of the population (in Israel, for example, the
crime rate is lower among observant Jews than among

---

*The profanation of God's name caused by unethical people who put
on the pretense of being religious, and the consequent alienation from
religion of irreligious people who might otherwise become religious is
underscored in the Talmud in the following declaration: ". . . if someone
studies Bible and Mishnah (the Oral Law) . . . but is dishonest in business and discourteous in his relations with people, what do people say
about him? 'Woe unto him who studies the Torah . . . This man studied
the Torah; look how corrupt are his deeds, how ugly his ways' " (*Yoma*
86a).

non-observant Jews) as where Jews constitute a minority.
Historically, the abhorrence of bloodshed among Jews is no
doubt largely attributable to Jewish law; and especially to
Kashrut which from ancient times generated among Jews
reverence for all life. For example, "consider the one
circumstance that no Jewish mother ever killed a chicken
with her own hand and you will understand why homicide is
rarer among Jews than among any other human group" (A.
Leroy Beaulieu, quoted in J.H. Hertz's commentary on the
Torah, London: 1972, p. 487).

2. More ethical behavior is (justifiably) expected from
observant Jews. Consequently we suspect that people are
more likely to recall instances of unethical behavior among
people considered to be religious. But it is well to bear in
mind the observation of Elie Wiesel concerning the behavior of rabbis in the concentration camps. "In the camps,
there were Capos (prisoners who worked for the Nazis) of
German, Hungarian, Czech, Slovakian, Georgian, Ukra-
nian, French and Lithuanian extraction. They were Christians, Jews and atheists. Former professors, industrialists,
artists, merchants, workers, militants from the right and
the left, philosophers and explorers of the soul, Marxists
and staunch humanists. And, of course, a few common
criminals. But not one Capo had been a rabbi" (Elie Wiesel,
One Generation After, New York, 1970, p. 189).

3. The possibilities of improving the moral conduct of
observant Jews is greater than the possibility of doing so
among the non-observant. Among observant Jews there
exists a religious/legal code to which one can appeal if one
wishes to improve their ethical conduct. Though they may
violate this code, at least they recognize it as binding since
it emanates from God. This fact was demonstrated during
the *Musar* (moral) movement within religious Jewish life in

the 19th century. The following tale concerning Rabbi
Israel Salanter, the founder of the *Musar* movement, is an
example of how the ethical behavior of a community of
observant Jews may be affected by an appeal to belief in
the Torah.

During the reign of Czar Nicholas I, young Jewish boys
were drafted into the Russian army for twenty-five years.
Local Jewish communities consequently passed regulations
to insure that as long as there was a family from which no
children had been taken, they would not conscript a second
child from any other family. Once, however, upon visiting a
city, Rabbi Salanter chanced upon a poor widow sobbing
bitterly. When he asked her the reason for her intense
sorrow, she responded that she had just been informed that
her second son was to be drafted because of the illegal
intervention of the *nagid* (wealthy man and a leader of the
community) who wished to insure that none of his children
would be taken. The rest of the community acquiesced and
decided that the two children of the defenseless widow be
drafted instead.

Salanter went that afternoon to the services at the local
synagogue, and when one man rose to lead the prayer
services, the Rabbi yelled at him, "It is forbidden for you to
lead us in prayer for you are not a believer in God and
Torah." A replacement was sent and Salanter shouted the
same thing at the second man. This happened yet a third
time and a fourth. Finally, the congregants asked Rabbi
Israel to explain his behavior. In essence he answered
them: "You are obviously not believers in the Torah. The
fact that you pray is itself irrelevant. You pray because
your fathers prayed. And how do I know that you are not
believers? If you believed in the Torah, and sincerely believed that it was the voice of God commanding you, then
how would you dare ignore the laws in the Torah which
forbid you to oppress a widow, or to favor prominent

people in a judgment? That you are willing to ignore such laws shows that you do not really believe that the Torah was God-given. Hence, you are non-believers."

In order to improve the ethical behavior of religious Jews, Rabbi Salanter was able to appeal to the Torah. Should we wish to raise the level of ethical behavior of non-observant Jews, however, to what generally recognized code of binding ethics can we appeal?

What is therefore most urgently needed today is a renewed commitment among observant Jews, and among their leaders in particular, to ethical excellence. The observant Jew must serve as a moral light to non-observant Jews just as all Jews must serve as an example to the non-Jewish world. *Imagine the effect it would have upon non-observant Jews if observant Jews were as identifiable by their commitment to ethical behavior as they are by their observance of Shabbat and Kashrut.*

As a final consideration it must be stressed that many in the religious community must bear much of the blame for the widespread impression that religious people are in no way ethically superior to the rest of the Jewish community. Too often the religious leadership and their followers have lent credibility to this impression by judging Jews solely by their observance of man-God laws, whereas a Jew should be judged according to the level of his commitment to *all* Mitzvot. As a result, these Jews have helped foster the erroneous and dangerous opinion that religion is irrelevant to ethics.

A number of reasons can be suggested to explain this sad development. One is the fact that while the religious community has always maintained communal institutions regulating rituals (e.g., rabbinic supervision of Kashrut), it has had to allow governmental regulations to prevail in the more obviously social and ethical realms. Thus one wishing to know whether a piece of meat is kosher will of course ask a rabbi, but if he wishes to know whether a given action is ethically kosher, he is far less likely to turn to his rabbi or to Jewish sources despite the fact that ethical issues are comprehensively legislated in Jewish codes of law. Unfortunately, many religious people have come to view their limited Judaism as constituting all of Judaism, and have consequently restricted their religious concerns to the realm of the ritual.*

A second factor responsible for the fact that moral concerns are not as great as they should be in the religious community is that Judaism is often transmitted to children not as a *moral* way of life but as meaningless habits which become a *social* way of life. Many children raised in observant environments come to observe Jewish laws not from an appreciation of the laws' moral and spiritual bases, but out of fear of what parents and neighbors would say if they were "caught" violating a law, and because their observance has become an ingrained habit. In either case they are not observing Jewish laws with the intention of becoming moral through them, and the laws therefore, cease to have the morally elevating effect which they are meant to have.

For these reasons there is a pressing need in the ob-

---

*It should be noted that there still are religious Jews who submit their business disputes to a rabbinic court, *Bet Din*, for adjudication. If both parties to the dispute agree to accept the ruling of the three rabbis, the decision will be upheld even in civil courts. My grandfather (J.T.), Rabbi Nissen Telushkin, of blessed memory, on a number of occasions sat as a rabbinical judge in cases involving tens of thousands of dollars. Even today, therefore, a Jew who is interested in conducting his business according to Jewish law has the opportunity to do so.

servant community today for a contemporary Musar-type movement—a renewed commitment to ethical excellence and an educational campaign to teach the ethical component in all of Jewish law (see Appendix B for an example of the emergence of such a movement).

HOW DO YOU ACCOUNT FOR ETHICAL PEOPLE WHO ARE NOT RELIGIOUS?

The ethics of an irreligious actively moral person* stem from one or more of three factors:
1) The moral legacy of religion;
2) The individual's innate, or "natural," goodness;
3) A secular ethical system (e.g., ethical humanism).

Though these factors are each admirable, none of them invalidates the need for a religious-ethical system, for they cannot attain two essential achievements of religious-ethical systems: the adoption of the ethical code by significant numbers of people (rather than by a handful of exceptional individuals), and the transmission of the ethical code to future generations in order to thereby insure the code's perpetuation.

The Moral Legacy of Religion

The foundations of both personal and social morality in the West are religious. Though a moral individual may himself be a non-believer, he acquired his moral values

---

*As regards the ethics of the passively moral person, i.e. one whose behavior consists primarily of "not hurting anyone" see pp. 26-29.

from his immediate ancestors who in all likelihood were believers and/or from Western civilization which adheres (or at least pays lip service) to values first formulated by Judaism and interpreted by Christianity. Thus, the ethical atheist is essentially living on dividends bequeathed by thousands of years of religious belief.

Consequently, we ask whether the moral atheist will be capable of bequeathing a moral legacy to his offspring now that he has cut them off from God, the ultimate source of morality.* The answer, as history has shown, is no. Except for a handful of righteous individuals, the legacy of ideologies which deny God's existence has been unparalleled human suffering.**

---

*For a discussion of why a moral system is impossible without God, see Question 1. The point is also developed by Professor Will Herberg: "The moral principles of Western civilization are, in fact, all derived from the tradition rooted in Scripture and have vital meaning only in the context of that tradition. The attempt made in recent decades by secularist thinkers to disengage these values from their religious context, in the assurance that they could live a life of their own as a 'humanistic' ethic, has resulted in what one writer has called our 'cut-flower' culture. Cut flowers retain their original beauty and fragrance, but only so long as they retain the vitality that they have drawn from their now severed roots; after that is exhausted, they wither and die. So with freedom, brotherhood, justice and personal dignity—the values that form the moral foundation of our civilization. Without the life-giving power of the faith out of which they have sprung, they possess neither meaning nor vitality. Morality ungrounded in God is indeed a house built upon sand, unable to stand up against the vagaries of impulse and the brutal pressures of power and self-interest" (*Judaism and Modern Man*, N.Y.: 1951, pp. 91-2).

**Auschwitz and the Gulag Archipelago are two logical and perhaps inevitable outgrowths of atheism. In light of twentieth century man's experience with atheist regimes the burden of proof is upon atheists to show that such horrors are not inevitable outgrowths of the denial of God.

Natural Goodness: Moral Geniuses

A second explanation of the existence of ethical non-be-lievers is the simple fact that nature produces a certain number of naturally good people—moral geniuses, we may call them—just as it occasionally produces artistic or scientific geniuses. But just as we cannot stop teaching music and rely on nature to produce Beethovens, we cannot stop teaching morals and rely upon nature to occasionally blossom forth moral geniuses. As music must be systematically taught to anyone who aspires to musical proficiency, so morality must be systematically taught to anyone who aspires to moral proficiency.*

Thus, because a) Judaism aims to transform Everyman morally, rather than just constitute the ethical philosophy of a handful of dedicated people, and because b) Judaism has always recognized that most people are not naturally good, moral geniuses, but that the "predilection of man's heart is evil from his youth" (*Genesis* 8:21)*. Judaism instituted a religious-ethical system by which anyone—and ultimately an entire society—can become godlike.

---

*The need for such a moral and ethical system is illustrated by the experience of Andrei Sakharov, the Soviet physicist, who has devoted his life to the fight for human rights. Sakharov is that exception among men whose morality can be characterized as "natural," rather than induced by any specific moral system. Yet Sakharov has apparently been unable to pass on his morality to his children, all of whom support the Soviet regime which oppresses their father. They are "normal" people, who without a systematic method of moral learning and practice, were unable to emulate their father.

**This recognition of the human predilection towards evil should in no way be confused with the non-Jewish doctrine of original sin. The individual, according to Judaism, is born morally clean. The Torah in *Genesis* 8:21 merely observes that which should be obvious to those of us who live after the revelations of Freudian psychology and the horrors of the twentieth century: that man's instincts, if not channeled in good' directions, will lead him to evil.

An Irreligious Ethical System

That there exist actively ethical people who affirm no religious beliefs we have no doubt. That there are actively ethical people whose ethics emanate from a secular ethical system, however, we seriously doubt, if for no other reason than no such system exists. Ethical humanism is not a *system*. The Humanist Manifesto and similar documents are *ideals (which more often than not simply echo Jewish ideals*—as well they should, since the Ethical Culture Foundation was founded by a *rabbi*, Felix Adler, in 1876) without God and without a systematic method of adoption by the individual or realization by a community.

CONCLUSION

To summarize, the existence of actively moral irreligious individuals in no way negates the need for a moral system, for one based on religious principles, and for a community of adherents to that system. Moreover, even with the best intentions, ethical atheists cannot be relied upon to perpetuate ethics since, in addition to the reasons cited in this answer, amorality is inherent to atheism. Milton Steinberg has written: ". . . how is one to account for the goodness of so many irreligionists? Very simply. Men often behave better than their philosophies. They cannot be expected to persist in doing so. In the end, how a man thinks must affect how he acts; atheism must finally, if not in one generation, then in several remake the conduct of atheists in the light of its own logic" (see *Anatomy of Faith*, N.Y., 1960, pp. 88-96).

Question 4

HOW DOES JUDAISM DIFFER FROM CHRISTIANITY, MARXISM AND COMMUNISM, AND ETHICAL HUMANISM?

These three movements have three things in common. Each was founded by a Jew, each is a derivative of Judaism seeking to fulfill the messianic and utopian goals which Judaism introduced, and each dropped the Jewish means for attaining these goals.

Part 1

CHRISTIANITY

Whether or not Jesus was the Messiah is not the most important question which divides Judaism and Christianity.

The major difference between Judaism and Christianity lies in the importance each religion attaches to faith and law.* In Judaism man is judged by God by his deeds, not by his faith;** according to the Bible, observance of the laws of the Torah is the Jews' central obligation. As Christianity developed, however, it did away with Biblical law, and consequently faith became its central demand.

---

*The question of whether or not Jesus was the Messiah prophesied in the Bible—the issue with which most discussions of Judaism and Christianity are concerned—will be discussed later.

**This consitutes one of the few beliefs in Judaism that are affirmed across the Jewish religious spectrum, from the most Reform to the most Orthodox. In any synagogue, on any Shabbat or holiday, the emphasis in the rabbi's sermon is almost always on deeds. The nature of the deeds being emphasized might differ: in the Reform synagogue there might be greater emphasis on social action, and in the Orthodox one on the proper observance of the Shabbat, though increasingly it could be the other way around. But it is *inconceivable* that a rabbi would deliver a sermon on salvation through faith, an extremely common subject of Christian sermons.

FAITH OVER WORKS:
ITS DEVELOPMENT IN CHRISTIANITY

Though faith became the essence of Christianity, Christian history reveals that this emphasis on faith over works was held neither by Jesus nor by his immediate followers. The New Testament bears witness to the fact that Jesus and his early followers stressed and observed Jewish law: "Do not imagine that I have come to abolish the Law or the Prophets," Jesus declared to his early disciples, "I tell you solemnly, till heaven and earth disappear, not one dot, not one little stroke, shall disappear from the Law (the Torah) until its purpose is achieved."* Jesus then concluded his message with a warning against anyone who violates Jewish law: "Therefore, the man who infringes even the least of these commandments and teaches others to do the same will be considered the least in the kingdom of heaven; but the man who keeps them and teaches them will be considered great in the kingdom of heaven" (*Matthew* 5:17-9).

After his death, Jesus' disciples continued to heed their teacher's message to observe Halakha (Jewish law). *Acts* 2:46 and 3:1 state that the disciples regularly prayed at the Temple; *Acts* 10:14 records Peter's scrupulous observance of Kashrut (the Jewish dietary laws); *Acts* 15:1 teaches that "some men came down from Judea" (these men, in line with *Galatians* 2:12, appear to have been sent by James, Jesus' brother) to teach that "unless you have yourselves been circumcised in the tradition of Moses, you cannot be

---

*The law's purpose is, of course, the arrival of the kingdom of heaven, the rule of God on earth, a goal which neither religion believes has been realized.

saved." In *Acts* 21:24, James says to Paul, . . . "let everyone know there is no truth in the reports they have heard about you, and that *you still regularly observe the Law.*" However, in the year 70, when the Jewish community in Jerusalem was destroyed by the Romans, a new ideology which opposed the attitude of Jesus and his disciples towards God's law became dominant in Christianity.

THE NEW IDEOLOGY

The formulator of this new ideology was Paul of Tarsus, and he theorized as follows:

a) *All* the laws of the Torah must be observed—therefore breaking one of them renders one cursed: ". . . *scripture says: Cursed be everyone who does not persevere in observing everything prescribed in the book of the Law*" *(Galatians* 3:10);

however,

b) man, being imperfect, will inevitably violate at least one law: "*We could have been justified by the Law if the Law we were given had been capable of giving life, but it is not: scripture makes no exceptions when it says that sin is master everywhere* . . ." *(Galatians* 3:21-2);

therefore:

c) man is cursed by the Law: ". . . *those who rely on the keeping of the Law are under a curse* . . ." *(Galatians* 3:10);

and

d) man must be redeemed from the Law, a redemption which can come *only* through belief in Jesus: "*Christ redeemed us from the curse of the Law* . . ." *(Galatians* 3:10), ". . . *we conclude that a man is put right with God only through faith and not by doing what the law commands*" *(Romans* 3:28).

JUDAISM'S DIFFERENCES WITH THIS IDEOLOGY

a) The Pauline idea that a person is cursed by God for breaking any law (see *Galatians* 3:10-3) was a new one, not to be found anywhere in the Bible or in normative Judaism. From where then did Paul develop this notion? It appears from *Galatians* 3:10 that he derived it from a mistaken reading of a verse in the Bible, *Deuteronomy* 27:26. *Deuteronomy* 27:15-25 list eleven basic ethical obligations (prohibitions against violence, bribery, idolatry, incest, oppression of the weak, etc.) and declare the transgressor of any of them to be cursed by the Jews and Moses (not by God). At the conclusion of these verses the Bible says, "Cursed be he who does not maintain all the words of *this* Torah to do them . . ." — "this Torah (Teaching)" referring to the eleven laws just listed. However, Paul understood this verse to mean, "Cursed be everyone who does not persevere in observing *everything* prescribed in *the book* of the Law" (as it is translated in *Galatians* 3:10). Paul misunderstood (or intentionally changed) the verse to mean that anyone who violates any law in the *entire* Torah (Five Books of Moses) is to be eternally cursed, a mistranslation which remains in the New Testament.*

b) The Bible appreciates that only perfect human beings can perfectly fulfill all its laws at all times, and it therefore understands that man will occasionally fail. Hundreds of

---

*Anyone familiar with Hebrew will immediately perceive the mistranslation. But one need not know Hebrew to understand Paul's error; a simple reading of *Deuteronomy* 27:15-26 makes it clear, since, among other reasons, a) there would have been no need to relist eleven commandments if *Deuteronomy* 27:26 referred to every law in the Torah, and b) the Hebrew Bible frequently uses the words "Torah" and "this Torah" in reference to a specific group of laws (for the term "Torah," see *Leviticus* 6:2; 6:18; 7:37; 11:46; 13:59; 14:2; 15:32, and *Numbers* 6:21; for the expression "this Torah" see *Deuteronomy* 1:5; 4:8; 28:61; 31:9, 11).

years before Paul, the Jews were assured that God recognizes that "there is no man so righteous who does only good
and never sins" (*Ecclesiastes* 7:20). Furthermore, the Bible
repeatedly tells of Jews who sinned (including Moses and
David) and who, after repenting and returning to observance of the law which they violated, were restored to
God's grace, certainly without being eternally cursed.*

c) Needless to say, Judaism does not want people to violate the law. But if a Jew does violate it, the law enables
him to return to God and right action through
repentance—in Hebrew, *teshuvah*, from the word for
"return." *Teshuvah* consists of three steps: the sinner must
recognize his sin, feel sincere remorse at having sinned,
and resolve to return to fulfilling the law. There was also a
fourth step during the time of the Temple—the bringing of
a sacrifice—but since the destruction of the Temple this
step has been unnecessary, *a fact long foreseen by the
Bible.* In the words of Hosea (14:3) prophesying of a time
when the Temple would no longer be standing, ". . . turn
to the Lord, say to Him, Forgive all inquity and receive us
graciously, *so we will offer the prayers of our lips instead of
calves.*" Hosea's statement is paralleled by *Proverbs* 21:3,
"To do righteousness and justice is more acceptable to God
than sacrifices," and by the book of *Jonah* which recounts
that when the people of Nineveh repented, their sins were

---

*The notion of men being cursed by God raises two other new issues,
hell and eternal damnation, concerning which it should be noted that *the
word hell never appears in the Hebrew Bible, and eternal damnation is
unknown to Judaism.* The Bible does speak of *sheol,* a Hebrew word
which has been mistranslated as "hell," but this word means "grave." In
Genesis 37:35, for example, Jacob speaks of going to *sheol,* his grave,
without seeing Joseph. Jacob, the Patriarch, did not say he was going to
hell. Also, the notion of a hell where sinners suffer eternally is foreign to
Judaism and entered Western man's religious consciousness through the
New Testament.

forgiven by God despite the fact that they brought no sin-offering.*

Finally, the doctrine that God would curse men whom He created imperfect for being imperfect is one which depicts God as cruel and sadistic,** notions utterly foreign to Judaism.

d) As we noted at the outset, Judaism judges a person by his actions rather than by his faith. The Talmud, basing itself on *Jeremiah* 16:11, stated: "Better that they (the children of Israel) abandoned me (God) and continued observing my laws," (because, the Talmud adds, through observance of the laws they will return to God—*Jerusalem Talmud, Hagiggah* 1:7).

Despite the Bible's emphasis on deed more than creed, however, Paul declared (*Romans* 3:28) that "we conclude that a man is put right with God only through faith and not by doing what the law commands."

Owing to the Pauline doctrine as formulated in *Romans*, the criterion by which Catholicism and Protestantism came to judge people was faith in Jesus. The Catholic Church held that salvation depended on faith plus sacraments; and the father of Protestantism, Martin Luther, differed from the Church not in stressing the need for good deeds, but in stressing that faith alone, without sacraments, was sufficient. In a pamphlet issued in 1520, Luther declared,

---

*There are numerous other Biblical passages referring to the possibility of forgiveness and redemption without sacrifices, e.g., *Leviticus* 26:40-5; *Deuteronomy* 4:29-31; *Jeremiah* 50:20; *Ezekiel* 22:15.

**This caricature of God which results from Paul's caricature of the law, is the major source of the pernicious myth which contrasts the "vengeful Jewish God of the Old Testament" with the "loving Christian God of the New Testament."

"Above all things bear in mind what I have said, that faith alone without works, justifies, sets free and saves" (*On Christian Liberty*).

As a result, the average Christian took *Romans* 3:28 to mean that in God's eyes, man's morality is less important than his beliefs, while many clerics used this statement as the ultimate rationale for persecuting people for their beliefs.

It may be objected that the Christians who have committed evil acts have misconstrued Paul. Perhaps they have, for Paul certainly advocated loving behavior.* The fact remains, however, that whereas the Bible did not regard Judaism as incumbent upon all people, and whereas in Judaism the righteous of all nations attain salvation (*Tosefta Sanhedrin* 13:2), in Christianity, Christ had to become the sole means to salvation since, as Paul reasoned, *if good deeds could achieve salvation, there would be no purpose to the crucifixion and "Christ would have died in vain" (Galatians 2:21).*

CHRISTIAN DOGMAS AND JUDAISM

Three major dogmas distinguish Christianity from Judaism: original sin, the Second Coming, and atonement through Jesus' death. *To Christians these beliefs are needed to solve otherwise insoluble problems. For Jews, however, these beliefs are not needed because these problems do not exist.*

---

*Though, as we wrote in Question 2, "Idealism is not enough . . . a detailed ethical system binding on every individual is indispensable to achieving universal peace, justice, and brotherhood."

1. **Problem:** Original Sin.
  Solution: Acceptance of Christ through baptism.

Paul wrote: "Sin came into the world through one man
. . . Then as one man's trespass led to condemnation for all
men, so one man's act of righteousness leads to acquittal
and life for all men. For as by one man's disobedience many
were made sinners, so by one man's obedience many will be
made righteous" (*Romans* 5:12, 18-19). Because original sin
tainted all men, a solution had to be found which could
justify men in the eyes of God. The baptismal solution was
confirmed in the "Decrees of the Council of Trent" (1545-
63): "since the Fall caused loss of righteousness, thralldom
to the devil and liability to the wrath of God, and since
original sin is transmitted by generation and not by imitation, *therefore, all which has the proper nature of sin,
and all guilt of original sin is removed in baptism*" (see
Encyclopedia of Religion and Ethics IX, p. 562).

In Judaism, however, original sin is not a problem since
such an idea does not exist. According to Judaism, man is
born untainted (cf. note on p. 66). He makes his own moral
choice to sin or not to sin.

2. **Problem:** Man cannot achieve salvation through his
  actions.
  Solution: Jesus' death atones for men's sins when they
have faith in him.* For Christians the sacrificial death of
Jesus solves the dilemma that man cannot achieve salvation
through his own actions.

---

*This belief raises a significant question: for what sins of mankind
was Jesus' death supposed to atone? Since the Bible did not oblige the
non-Jewish world to obey Jewish laws between man and God, they could
not have sinned in this area. The only sins which mankind could have
committed were between man and man, the ethical laws. Does the
Pauline doctrine mean that Jesus died to atone for man's sins against his

The solution is irrelevant to Judaism because it never ceased maintaining that the law must be observed, since even if Jesus were the one man who fulfilled the law perfectly, this would still not justify his followers' rejection of it.*

3. **Problem:** The Messianic prophecies were not fulfilled when Jesus came.

    Solution: The Second Coming.

For Christians a second coming is necessary so that Jesus can fulfill the Messianic prophecies which he did not fulfill. Jewishly speaking, there is no problem since the Jews never had reason to believe that Jesus was the Messiah (see p. 81ff.), and the Bible never mentioned a second Messianic coming.

---

fellow man? If so, the ethical upshot of this doctrine is perilous. This doctrine opposes the Jewish doctrine that forgiveness for sins against one's fellow man is not in God's hands, but only in the hands of the offended human being. Moreover, the Christian position that Jesus' life and death absolved us from observing the laws between man and God is also morally questionable since it is not always possible to differentiate between laws between man and God and ethical laws. One of the purposes of Kashrut, for example, was to insure that animals were slaughtered as painlessly as possible. To the animal kingdom's misfortune, Christianity dropped Kashrut because it considered it to be only a law between man and God.

*The notion that Jesus freed future men from observing Jewish law makes as little sense, Jewishly speaking, as the idea that one man's perfect observance of traffic laws would free future men from obeying traffic laws. In Judaism, as in all legal systems, it is a basic principle that after one repents for violation of a law, one must return to observing the law. The purpose of sacrifice and repentance was to obtain forgiveness for the past, not to serve as a dispensation from practicing the law in the future. Furthermore, even if one assumes that through Jesus' death we receive God's forgiveness for violating laws, why are we then free from observing them?

JESUS AND JUDAISM

It should surprise no one to learn that many of Jesus' statements parallel Biblical and Pharisaic beliefs, since Jesus generally observed rabbinic (Pharisaic) Judaism. There are, however, a number of innovative teachings attributed to Jesus in the New Testament—it is of course impossible to know whether these statements were actually uttered by him, or merely attributed to him—and we will briefly indicate what some of these teachings are and how Judaism differs from them.

1. Jesus forgives sins in his own name: "The Son of man has the authority to forgive sins." (*Matthew* 9:6). Judaism believes to the contrary that God Himself is limited in His power to forgive sins, for He can only forgive those sins committed against Himself. As the Mishnah teaches: "The Day of Atonement atones for sins against God, not for sins against man, unless the injured party has been appeased," (*Yoma* 8:9).

2. Jesus' law of love: "Love your enemies and pray for your persecutors" (*Matthew* 5:44) and "offer the wicked man no resistance. On the contrary, if anyone hits you on the right cheek, offer him the other as well" (*Matthew* 5:38-9). Judaism, in contrast, does not demand that one love one's enemies—though it is completely untrue to claim as Matthew does that Judaism commands one to hate his enemies (see *Matthew* 5:43)—but it does command that one act with justice and compassion towards one's enemies. For example, "If you see the donkey of one that hates you lying under its burden, and he is having difficulty in removing the burden, you must help him unload it" (*Exodus* 23:5). A Jew is therefore commanded to act with justice towards all men; but a Jew is not, for example, commanded to love a Nazi as the statement in Matthew demands.* And the idea that one should "offer the wicked man no resistance"

opposes the Biblical commandment "you shall burn the evil out from your midst" (*Deuteronomy* 7:17).

3. The Christian belief that men can come to God only through Jesus, "No one knows the Father except the Son and anyone to whom the Son chooses to reveal him" (*Matthew* 11:27), differs from the Jewish belief that every man has equal and direct access to God, for "God is near to all who call unto Him" (*Psalms* 145:18). Judaism denies the need for intermediaries between man and God, and to this day the rabbi performs no function that cannot be performed by any educated layman.

4. Jesus' attitude towards non-Jews: see *Matthew* 15:22-8 and compare it with the *Second Book of Kings* 5:1ff. and the book of *Jonah*.

WHY DO JEWS NOT ACCEPT JESUS AS THE MESSIAH?

Judaism does not believe that Jesus was the Messiah because he did not fulfill any Messianic prophecies. The major prophecy concerning the Messianic days is that "Nation shall not lift up sword against nation, nor shall they learn war anymore" (*Isaiah* 2:4; see also *Isaiah* 2:1-3; 11:1-10). Universal peace must accompany the Messiah,

---

*In stress situations, Jesus himself seems to have found it difficult to follow this principle (e.g., *Matthew* 10:32, 25:41), and virtually no Christian group has ever found it possible to utilize this principle in directing its practical policy. Nor is this a moral ideal. One of the few Christian groups to incorporate 'offer the wicked man no resistance' into its everyday life—the Jehovah's Witnesses—was used in the concentration camps as barbers by SS men confident that the Jehovah's Witnesses would do nothing to harm them or other Nazi mass murderers (see *Mauthausen* by Evelyn Le Chene, Fakenham, Norfolk, Great Britain: 1971, p. 130).

and should peace not come, the Messiah has obviously not. The Talmud records that in the second century, Rabbi Akiva, the greatest rabbi of his age, believed that Simon Bar Kochva was the Messiah. Yet when Bar Kochva's revolt against the Romans was crushed, Rabbi Akiva recognized that Bar Kochva could not have been the Messiah, though he was still regarded as an essentially righteous man, because the Messiah, according to the Bible, will establish peace for all mankind and gain sovereignty for the Jews.

It has been obvious for over 1900 years that the Messianic days of peace have not arrived, yet Christians still contend that Jesus was the Messiah. What is the Christian explanation? There will be, according to Christianity, a second coming, at which time Jesus will fulfill the Messianic functions originally expected of him. For Judaism, however, this explanation is unsatisfactory; the idea of a second coming is nowhere to be found in the Bible. In fact, it appears likely that this idea was not even known to Jesus himself, for he told his followers that some of them would yet be alive when all the Messianic prophecies would materialize (*Mark* 9:1; 13:30). This idea of a second coming was apparently formulated by later Christians to explain Jesus' failure to fulfill his Messianic prophecies.

Concerning the other Messianic prophecies, David Berger, a scholar in the field and Assistant Professor of History at the City University of New York, has written: ". . . we have overwhelming evidence that the Messiah has not come, and against this evidence we are confronted by a dubious collection of isolated verses, forcibly wrenched out of context and invariably misinterpreted."

A primary example of such misinterpretation is the translation and meaning which Christians have given to *Isaiah* 7:14, "Behold a young woman (*almah*) shall conceive . . ." In *Matthew* 1:22-3 the verse was changed to read "a virgin shall conceive," and for nearly two thousand years this was cited as proof that the virgin birth of Jesus was prophesied in the Bible. But *almah* does not mean virgin; the Hebrew word for virgin is *betulah* (see *Leviticus* 21:3; *Deuteronomy* 22:19; 23:28; and *Ezekiel* 44:22). Had Isaiah wished to prophesy that a virgin shall conceive, he would have used this word. The context in which the passage occurs also renders the Christological meaning untenable. The verses in Isaiah describe events that Ahaz (a king of Judah in the time of Isaiah) was expected to witness, 700 years before Jesus.*

Fortunately, in recent years Christian scholars have also begun to acknowledge the illegitimacy of attempts to prove Jesus' Messiahship from the Hebrew Bible. J.C. Fenton in his *The Gospel of St. Matthew* (Baltimore: 1963, p. 17f.) wrote: "It is now seen that the Old Testament was not a collection of detailed foretellings of future events, which could only be understood centuries later: the Old Testament writers were in fact writing for their contemporaries in a way which could be understood by them, and describing things that would happen more or less in their own lifetime. Thus Matthew's use of the Old Testament . . . is now a stumbling-block to the twentieth century reader of his Gospel." The well-known Christian scholar and theologian W.C. Davies likewise notes that the

---

*Another example of Christian misinterpretation is the use of *Isaiah* 53 as a Christological reference. Professor Eliezer Berkovits of the Hebrew Theological College has written: "God's chosen people is the suffering servant of God. The majestic fifty-third chapter of Isaiah is the description of Israel's martyrology through the centuries [and] the way Christianity treated Israel through the ages only made Isaiah's description fit Israel all the more tragically and truly. Generation after generation Christians poured out their iniquities and inhumanity over the head of Israel, yet they "esteemed him, stricken, smitten of God, and afflicted" (*Faith After the Holocaust*, New York: 1973, pp. 125-6).

Gospels quote the Old Testament selectively: "There were some prophecies which they ignore and others which they modify" ("Torah and Dogma—A Comment," *Harvard Theological Review*, April 1968, p. 99). Another Christian scholar, R. Taylor, noted in his commentary on *Psalms* 16:8-10 in *The Interpreter's Bible* that the New Testament interpretation misreads the clear intention of the Psalmist.

In sum, Jesus did not fulfill the prophecies of the Bible which Judaism expects the Messiah to fulfill. Hence, Jews and Judaism do not believe him to have been the Messiah.

CONCLUSION

As we have seen, there are significant differences between Judaism and Christianity. The existence of such differences, however, should serve as no barrier to the development of close relationships between Jews and Christians. As Trude Weiss-Rosmarin, author of the excellent *Judaism and Christianity—The Differences* (New York: 1943) has written: "The notion that Judaism and Christianity, to maintain harmonious relations, must be 'truly, basically one,' is really a totalitarian aberration. For democracy is predicated on the conviction that dissimilarities and differences are no cause or justification for inequality. . . . After all, we don't demand that all Americans vote for the same ticket in order to promote national unity" (pp. 11-12).

Dr. Weiss-Rosmarin's last point is a crucial one. While we must not demand that all Americans vote for the same party, we do feel it legitimate to demand that all Americans feel committed to the democratic process. Once this shared appreciation for democracy exists there is room for disagreement. The same is true today of the world at large. There are two basic competing camps in today's world, those who follow a materialist interpretation of reality, and for whom morality is relative, and those who hold that there is a God transcending material reality from Whom emanates one standard of morality. This is the basic belief that unites all men of religion; and just as we presuppose a commitment to the democratic process on the part of Republicans and Democrats so we presuppose that Christians and Jews are united in regarding God's law as the higest law.

We need discussions today between Jews and Christians to formulate a program of action to fulfill the religious man's role of "perfecting the world under the rule of God." The Western world is sinking into moral relativism, materialism, hedonism and secularism. Our dialogue must therefore be motivated not by a desire to convert each other, but by a desire to convert a secular world into a religious one.

Part 2

MARXISM AND COMMUNISM

Right can never be higher than the economic structure of society and the cultural development thereby determined. We therefore reject every attempt to impose on us any moral dogma whatsoever as an eternal, ultimate and forever immutable moral law . . . all former moral theories are the product, in the last analysis, of the economic stage which society has reached at that particular epoch.

Karl Marx, *Capital*

We say that our morality is entirely subordinated to the interests of the class struggle of the proletariat . . . We do not believe in an eternal morality . . . We repudiate all morality derived from non-human (i.e., God) and non-class concepts.

Vladimir Ilyich Lenin

. . . for Marxism there is no reason (literally no reason: our universe, the movement posits, is the kind of universe where there cannot conceivably be any reason) for not killing or torturing or exploiting a human person if his liquidation or torture or slave labor will advance the historical process.

Professor Wilfred Cantwell Smith (McGill University), *Islam in Modern History*

"You shall do no unrighteousness in judgment; you shall not respect the person of the poor [worker], nor favor the powerful [capitalist] but in righteousness you shall judge your neighbor."

Leviticus 19:15

MARXISM AND COMMUNISM

1. Motivating Aims

Marxism and Judaism are both motivated by the desire to ultimately perfect this world and establish a Utopia on earth. It was Judaism which first brought the utopian and messianic vision to mankind, from God's promise to Abraham the first Jew, "Through you all the families of the earth will be blessed" (*Genesis* 12:3), to the Prophets' unique expressions of universal brotherhood and peace, such as Isaiah's call to nations to "beat their swords into plowshares."

Marxism, a secular offshoot of Judaic religious universalism, also calls for universal peace and brotherhood, and it is precisely in this context that the messianism and utopianism of Karl Marx become explicable. The thinking of this grandson of two Orthodox rabbis was rooted in Jewish moral fervor. As the (non-Jewish) scholar Edmund Wilson wrote in his history of socialism: "The characteristic genius of the Jew has been especially a moral genius. . . . Nobody but a Jew (i.e., Marx) could have fought so uncompromisingly and obstinately for the victory of the dispossessed classes" (*To The Finland Station*, Garden City, New York: 1953, p. 307).

Thus, it is not to their motivating aims that one must look to find the essential differences between Marxism and Judaism.

2. The System

This is the second area in which there are more similarities than differences between Marxism and Judaism. Both are all-encompassing world-views in theory and practice. In fact, they may both be called religions.

Since it should come as no surprise that we would characterize Judaism as a religion (though it is not solely one), let us explain our use of the word "religion" with reference to Marxism.

To the believing Marxist, Marxism is a religion. It has its own god (man), prophet (Marx), apostles (Lenin, Stalin, Mao, and others, depending on the sect), dogma (dialectical materialism), absolute (science), ethic (proletarian solidarity), utopian visions, all-embracing answers, community of believers, traditions, schisms, and even churches (first Moscow, and since the Chinese Reformation, Peking and other smaller churches). "The religious essence of Marxism is superficially obscured by Marx's rejection of the traditional religions. . . . Like medieval Christianity, Marx's system undertakes to provide an integrated, all-inclusive view of reality, an organization of all significant knowledge in an interconnected whole, a frame of reference within which all possible questions of importance are answered or answerable" (Robert Tucker, *Philosophy and Myth in Karl Marx*, Cambridge: 1961, p. 22).

Their similar goals and types of organization notwithstanding, Marxism and Judaism are as opposed as any two religions can possibly be.

3. The Highest Being

Their most obvious difference concerns God and man. Whereas for Judaism, "God is the Lord, there is none other," for Marx, "the highest being for man is man himself."* Man is god, and conversely, according to Engels,

---

*Karl Marx, "Zur Kritik der Hegelschen Rechtphilosophie," in Marx and Engels *Der historische Materialismus; Die Fruhschriften*, (Leipzig: 1932, I), p. 272; cited in Alfred G. Meyer, *Marxism, The Unity and Theory of Practice*, Ann Arbor: 1963, p. 51.

"God is man."** Moreover, the Marxist Man/god is also a jealous god who tolerates no other gods; Marx wrote that "human self-consciousness . . . (is) . . . the supreme divinity—by the side of which none other shall be held."*** As the Jewish God transcends man and also tolerates no other gods, the lines of battle between Marxism and Judaism would seem to be clearly drawn. But, as we shall now see, this difference alone is much less significant than its consequences.

4. Morality

Marxism denies the existence of God. It affirms only the existence of matter (and of man since he is composed of matter), and as we have seen in Question 1, when God is denied and matter is the one reality, morality is relative and therefore objectively nonexistent. For this reason, Marxists from Marx to Lenin to Mao have all agreed that morality is relative (to the class), that *all revolutionary behavior is morally justified*, and that to oppose such behavior is to suffer from "bourgeois morality."

"Right can never be higher than the economic structure of society and the cultural development thereby determined," wrote Marx. "We therefore reject every attempt to impose on us any moral dogma whatsoever as an eternal, ultimate and forever immutable moral law on the pretext that the moral world too has its permanent prin-

---

**Marx and Engels, *MEGA (Historische-Kritische Gesamtausgabe)* II, p. 428, cited in Tucker, *op. cit.*, p. 73.

***Marx and Engels, *MEGA* I part 1, p. 10, cited in Tucker, *op. cit.*, p. 74.

ciples which transcend history and the differences between nations. We maintain on the contrary that all former moral theories are the product, in the last analysis, of the economic stage which society had reached at that particular epoch."

To this Lenin added: "We say that our morality is entirely subordinated to the interests of the class struggle of the proletariat. . . . We do not believe in an eternal morality. . . . We repudiate all morality derived from nonhuman (i.e., God) and nonclass concepts" (Address to the Third Congress of the Russian Young Communist League, October 2, 1920).

In no area of life is the total opposition of Marxism to Judaism so apparent as in morality. Marxist morality sanctions any act so long as that act was committed "in the interests of the class struggle." The line between Marx and the Gulag Archipelago is direct, and with the benefit of hindsight, inevitable. Dropping "class enemies" into vats of acid (see Solzhenitsyn, *Gulag Archipelago*) is not an immoral act for Communists. By what Communist code of morality could such actions be morally condemned?

Judaism, which gave the world one God and one moral standard, recognizes no such relativization of morality. "You shall do no unrighteousness in judgment; you shall not respect the person of the poor [worker], nor favor the powerful [capitalist] but in righteousness you shall judge your neighbor" (*Leviticus* 19:15); "Woe unto them who call evil good and good evil" (*Isaiah* 5:20); "Love thy neighbor as thyself, I am God (who commands this)" (*Leviticus* 19:18). Personal moral behavior is the essence of Judaism; it is irrelevant to Marxism. The objection that Stalin was an aberration, or in the Marxist dialect a "deviationist," may be true in relation to his economic policies—but this argument is morally untenable. First, there is *nothing* in Marxism which would declare immoral the torture or murder of working-class enemies (and who, we ask, is to decide who these enemies are?). Only if one holds that morality transcends economic, national and individual inclinations can such actions be declared immoral. But a morality "which transcends history and the differences between nations" is precisely what Marx rejects. Second, Stalin only expanded the terror which Lenin began. The one exception proves this rule: "In his *Left-wing Communism, an Infantile Disorder* (1920), Lenin condemned terrorism (e.g., political assassination) because the Bolsheviks held at the time that it weakened the proletarian movement by encouraging the masses to believe that the revolution could be won for them by a few 'heroic individuals' instead of carrying it out for themselves. But he was careful to point out that his objection was 'of course only based on considerations of expediency', and Marxists have long since been permitted to use such methods if they are likely to be successful" (R.N. Carew Hunt, "The Ethics of Marxism" in *Marxism*, edited by Michael Curtis, New York: 1970, pp. 109-110). Third, during Stalin's lifetime, virtually all people who considered themselves Marxists continued to revere Stalin as a true Marxist. It was only years after Stalin had exterminated 18 million people that *factors external to the issue of Stalin's morality* caused some Marxists to denounce him. In any case, this mass murderer is still revered by the Chinese Communist Party which keeps his portrait on display in the Politburo. The North Vietnamese Communist Party also continues to adulate Stalin, a fact made apparent by its glorification of the Munich massacre of Israeli athletes as a "heroic revolutionary act." Moreover, during Stalin's reign of terror, Marxists found nothing in the writings of Karl Marx that would cause them to denounce Stalin's morality.

The upshot of the Marxist denial of one morality is the disappearance not only of morality but of freedom as well. As Professor Henry Bamford Parkes has observed: "The doctrine that all ideals and all values are socially determined leads . . . to the destruction of individual freedom and to the tyranny of the collectivity or of its embodiment in a dictator. Only the belief in objective rational truths and moral values can preserve freedom; for it is only through the right of appeal to objective standards that men can judge the actions of their government and resist them when they believe them to be wrong" (*Marxism: An Autopsy*, University of Chicago; 1939, p. 177).

5. Determinant of Man's Behavior

According to Marx, economics determines human history. Accordingly, one must look to economic forces to find the source of antisocial behavior. People commit evil acts as a direct consequence of their position in the class structure of society. Socio-economic conditions are responsible for human behavior.

Though Judaism is well aware of the importance of economics* and society, it holds individuals rather than society responsible for their actions. Men create society, and in an evil society, they are expected to rise above it. *Men, not socio-economic forces, built Auschwitz.* It is to underscore this very point that the Bible begins with two morality

---

*As examples, the Torah legislated against monopolies and protected the rights of those who had become bankrupt (*Leviticus* 25:8-28); and the Talmud put limitations on permissible profits (*Bava Mezia* 50b) and discouraged any attempts to corner the market in important commodities (*Bava Bathra* 90b and *Yoma* 83a). Vast portions of the Bible, the Talmud, and the codes of Jewish law are concerned with defining permissible business behavior.

tales. First it tells of the second two men in history, Cain and Abel, and portrays one of them as a murderer! One major point of this story is that evil comes from *within* the human being; no society existed which could have corrupted the second man in the world. Next, the Bible relates the tale of Noah, the one moral man in the world and therefore the only one spared by God in the flood. Every person in the world was held responsible for his or her unethical behavior despite the fact that the entire world, excluding Noah, was unethical.

6. Ways to Achieve Perfection

The results of these opposing views on the responsibility for evil individuals and an evil world are the two religions' different methods of eliminating evils. Since to Marxism economics determines history and the evil therein, the existing socio-economic order must be overthrown. Thus the Marxist must busy himself with hastening the revolution.

Judaism aims to solve the problem of an unjust world, but it rejects revolution as the panacea since *the roots of evil, injustice, etc. lie not in economics or society but in man himself.* Consequently, Judaism is a system designed to cause a moral revolution within each of its adherents before it and they can ever hope to succeed in perfecting the world. This is admittedly a considerably slower, hence less romantic, process than fomenting revolutions, and many people find its demands too restrictive compared with the personal moral anarchy of revolution-making. But Judaism's method happens to be infinitely more effective in achieving its results, for as most revolutions against tyranny have shown, when revolutionaries attain power they are at least as cruel as their predecessors. Why shouldn't they be? Do "revolutionaries" have higher standards of personal morality? There is simply no reason to trust that most revolutions will achieve *moral* results (we do not deny the probability of political and economic changes) since the people acceding to power are inherently no better than those they replace. When they have power, revolutionaries will act as all men without one moral standard will act: corruptly. Thus the descent from the high ideals of Marx to the brutality of Lenin, Trotsky, Stalin, Khrushchev and Brezhnev should surprise no one. Such a descent is virtually inevitable in any system that lacks, as Marxism does, personal moral responsibility.

7. **Man**

At this point it should be obvious even to the reader otherwise unacquainted with Judaism or Marxism what position each religion holds concerning the nature of man. Since Marxism maintains that socio-economic forces are responsible for the evil that people commit, and since the solution to antisocial behavior is revolution, Marxism must proceed from the assumption that men are basically good. It could be no other way, for if Marx were to assume that men would do evil irrespective of their economic position, his theories would crumble; they would be worthless as a guide to perfecting the world.

To "scientifically" substantiate the thesis that human nature is naturally good, Engels wrote in 1884 *The Origins of the Family, Private Property and the State*. The book, based upon the now discredited writings of the American anthropologist Lewis Morgan, purported to show that original man was really a wonderful fellow who became corrupt only with the advent of technology. Ancient man, according to this work, lived in a sort of ideal primitive communist society wherein cooperation and non-exploitation were the rules of life and mankind was one big happy family. Until the advent of technology, classes, and "self-alienating labor," man lived in his primitive goodness, a state of goodness which can return only once man returns to himself by means of the "inevitable" revolution. Thus, man being essentially good and "free" (see below), it is not man but his environment which must be changed.

Concerning man's innate goodness or lack of it, Judaism is quite explicit. Among the Torah's first descriptions of man is God's statement that "the predilection of man's heart (or id) is evil from his youth" (*Genesis* 8:21).* This does not mean that Judaism believes man to be inherently evil, but rather that *without correctives man will generally choose the easier course, which usually hurts other people.* We must be educated and disciplined to do what is good. Man needs correctives in order to channel his id or productive powers creatively, for good rather than evil. "Man has a poison in him," says the Talmud, "and the Torah [Halakha] is the antidote" (*Kiddushin* 30b).

Marx lived during the era when men were drunk with optimism. The nineteenth century Western liberal worshipped himself; it was the age of Prometheus unbound. We who live after Freudian revelations, Auschwitz and the Gulag Archipelago, and daily reports of sadism and wanton cruelty, reject naive belief in the "noble savage."

Modern man is not regarded by Judaism as inherently any different from primitive man. We all have the capacity to be Cain. Each person must struggle with weakness as if he or she were the first person on the earth. Judaism is geared to changing the individual and thereby the world and *as individuals have not changed, the values of Judaism are not time, class or nationality based but universal.*

---

*Man's creation "in the image of God" does not mean that man is basically good. It means that man, unlike animals, has the knowledge of good and evil, and can therefore *become* like God.

While Marxists may posit that man is good and needs no correctives, they have little compassion for man. If we are basically good, and if factors beyond our control cause us to act in a certain way, how do Marxists sanction hurting "class enemies" whose only fault is their having been born into the wrong class?

We also might ask: How good is man if all it takes is economics to drive him to commit evil? How do Marxists account for totally different ethical behavior among different people in the same economic class and circumstances? The answer is that for Marxism individuals have no importance. As G.D.H. Cole noted, for Marx "not individuals but only social classes possess ultimate reality" (*Capital, Introduction*, p. xxviii; cited in Tucker, p. 221).

According to Judaism, man must make himself good; according to Marxism man need not do anything to make himself good.

8. **Freedom**

Both religions revolve to a large extent around their conceptions of freedom. Yet these conceptions differ profoundly.

For Marxism, which conceives of the world in materialist terms, freedom is defined solely on a materialist level. Freedom is liberation from servitude; it is the workers' loss of their chains. ". . . the realm of freedom does not commence until the point is passed where labor under the compulsion of necessity and of external utility is required," Marx wrote in *Capital* (Chicago: 1933, Vol. III, p. 954).

To anyone familiar with Judaism, it hardly needs to be stressed how crucial a role freedom plays in it. Jewish history can be said to have begun with the Jews' liberation from Egypt, "the house of bondage," and the Shabbat, as well as Passover, is based on the theme of liberation. But Judaism does not regard liberation from external servitude

as "the realm of freedom," but only as one of two aspects of
freedom. There are two distinct aspects of freedom, external and internal; and once liberation from external servitude takes place, one must then liberate oneself from
internal domination, the domination of one's life by pas-
sions, needs, irrationality, etc. Thus, the ancient Jews
were not considered fully liberated even after their escape
from Egypt; they were only externally free. Only with the
receiving of the Law at Sinai could they embark on the
difficult process of attaining full freedom: "A man is not
free unless he involves himself in the Law," writes the
Talmud (*Ethics of the Fathers* 6:2).

In the well-chosen words of Princeton University Professor Robert Tucker, *"the only problem freedom can solve
is bondage;* otherwise it represents not a solution but
merely an opportunity. The real . . . emergence of man . . .
into adulthood, will only take place if this opportunity is
realized and worthy solutions of the problem of human
existence in freedom are found." (Tucker, *op. cit.*, p. 237,
emphasis ours).

Tucker's words precisely echo Judaism's view of freedom. Judaism is not content with external liberation; it is
equally preoccupied with "worthy solutions of the problem
of human existence in freedom."

But this is not the Marxist view. All man needs
according to Marx, is external liberation, since "freedom
. . . is the essence of man . . . No man fights against freedom" ("Debate on the Liberty of the Press," *Rheinische
Zeitung*, 12 May 1842). How then would Marx explain the
massive "escape from freedom," to use the famous words of
Erich Fromm, which has typified twentieth century man?
He never had to; he was living during the century of belief
in man.

We know now, however, that those who believe "the
essence of man is freedom," and that he therefore needs no

internal controls, have produced societies for less free than those who have understood that "the predilection of man's heart is evil from his youth" and who therefore recognized the need for self-discipline and internal liberation. Alexis de Tocqueville prophesied correctly: "He who seeks in Liberation anything other than Liberty itself is destined for servitude."

So long as we continue to think of freedom solely in terms of external liberation and continue to ignore the necessity for internal controls, there is not the slightest chance that world or personal violence will diminish, or that freedom will increase.

Finally, one must question the entire Marxian notion of human freedom. If indeed man is determined by his class and economic circumstances, how free is man? If we are so helpless in the face of economic forces are we really "free in essence?"

Just as, according to Judaism, men must work at making themselves good, so too must they work at making themselves free. Marxism sees no such need.

CONCLUSION

If Marxism were only an economic philosophy, there would be no need to contrast it with Judaism. Judaism has no quarrel with any economic system so long as it is moral. A good Jew can live in a capitalist society or in a socialist society (such as the religious kibbutzim in Israel).

But the Jewish issue with Marxism and Communism is not economic, it is moral. Marxism is not just an economic view, it is an all-embracing "scientific," religious, philosophical, moral, political, world-view. Every student of Marxism knows the issue is not Marxism and Communism vs. capitalism, but matter vs. transcendence, determinism vs. freedom, relative morality* vs. one morality, man as supreme vs. man under God.

The issues separating Judaism and Marxism are so great and numerous that we would characterize the ultimate battle in the contemporary world as one between Moses and Marx.

---

*"This growth of moral relativism is the most alarming tendency in both the theory and the political practice of the modern world; and though it is the Fascist states which have carried it to its most pernicious extreme, it originated—it is worthy of remark—with the Marxists. By interpreting all cultural phenomena in terms of class struggle, by explaining all the beliefs of every individual by his role in that struggle, by proclaiming that any means whatever are justified in achieving the end, and that the only predestined historic end is the conquest of power by the proletariat, Marxism subordinates man to the march of history and ennobles tyranny, dishonesty, cruelty, and mass murder" (Henry Bamford Parkes, *Marxism: An Autopsy*, University of Chicago: 1939, pp. 177-8).

Part 3

ETHICAL HUMANISM

A third option for persons interested in a better world is ethical humanism. This philosophy appeals to many individuals who though despairing of God and organized religion, remain committed to the ideal of ethical behavior. Underlying this philosophy is the assumption that we do not need God or religion to be ethical.

Because we have dealt in detail with the issues of God and morality, the need for an organized religious-ethical system, and the reasons for ethical people who are not religious in Questions 1, 2, and 3, our discussion here will be brief. If the reader has not already done so, he is asked to first read those three answers, and the second part of Question 3 in particular.

Since both ethical humanism and Judaism aim to create an ethical world, the most important question is: which is more likely to realize this aim, ethical humanism or ethical monotheism?

For the following reasons, most of which have been developed elsewhere in this book, it would seem clear that Judaism would constitute the more effective ethical system.

1. Ethical Humanism either holds that

a) morality is relative, in which case everyone is free to choose the morality that he or she prefers, and morality is, therefore, non-existent (see pp. 8-13),

or

b) there *are* moral absolutes, in which case the humanist has simply substituted *his* own absolutes for religious absolutes based upon God.

2. Since it denies the existence of God, humanism derives its moral ideals from man. But from which man? the brightest? the most rational? the leader? the majority? The humanist answers that "moral values derive their source from human experience" (*Humanist Manifesto* II, issued in 1973).

But who is to interpret this experience for all of us? Or is everyone to interpret it for himself? Humanists usually argue that the latter is the case. But how then can one standard of morality be established?

3. To this question the humanist responds that *reason* will establish morality. Reason is the humanists' arbiter of good and evil; it is the humanists' God and religion: "Rationality, or the attempt at it," writes Brand Blanshard, Professor of Philosophy at Yale, in a recent issue of *the Humanist* (November-December 1974), "takes the place of faith. . . . Take reason seriously. . . . Let it shape belief and conduct freely. It will shape them aright if anything can."

As we have seen (pp. 10-11), the belief that reason alone leads to moral behavior is itself irrational. If there is no single moral standard and morality is a matter of opinion, reason leads to nothing conclusive.

a) Reason can be used to justify any morality and any

crime.* As we noted in Question 1, "The use of reason to justify what is wrong is so common that we have a special word for it—rationalization."

b) Reason often conflicts with morality since morality often demands conduct which opposes reasonable self-interest. Though it was the moral thing to do, few people in Nazi occupied Europe found it reasonable to oppose Nazi atrocities—and those who did obeyed a morality higher than reason.

4. In addition to reason, humanists place great faith in education. As one humanist, Sigmund Freud, wrote in Vienna in 1927: "Civilization has little to fear from educated people and brain-workers. In them the replacement of religious motives for civilized behavior by other, secular motives, would proceed unobtrusively. . . ." (*The Future of an Illusion*, Garden City: 1964, p. 63).

As Dr. Freud was to witness within ten years of his making this statement, civilization has as much to fear from educated people and brain-workers as from the uneducated classes who Freud assumed were inherently less moral (*Ibid.*). Freud's fellow Austrian and German intellectuals showed no more moral strength than any other group of Germans and Austrians. Many of them not only supported Nazism, but as is indicated by the record of the German Medical Association and the evidence cited in Max Weinreich's *Hitler's Professors* (New York: 1946), also participated in its atrocities.

---

*To reasonable men of ancient Greece, reason dictated that unhealthy babies be left unattended to die. In the twentieth century, many inheritors of this Greek tradition of reliance on reason thought it reasonable to support Fascism or Communism. Reason can justify almost any behavior.

Nor did many intellectuals in the democracies exhibit much more moral acuity. As regards Western intellectual support of Stalin, for example, Professor George Watson of Cambridge University has written: "The published evidence alone demonstrates that many Western intellectuals in the age of Stalin *believed in extermination* in the sense of wanting it to happen" ("Were the Intellectuals Duped?" *Encounter*, December 1973; emphasis ours).

We therefore again ask the humanist: Upon whom or what can we rely to decide morality?

5. Humanism places great faith in man and progress, and obviously considers man to be basically very good—otherwise why be a humanist?

But does the evidence of human history (particularly in the twentieth-century societies that placed man over God—Nazi Germany, the Soviet Union and other Communist states) warrant this humanist optimism in the nature of undisciplined man?* After the butchery of this century and the massive horrors of history, is not the humanist's leap of faith to the innate goodness and reasonableness of man more irrational than the Jew's leap of faith to God and human holiness?

6. Humanism speaks of no ethical ideals which Judaism has not advocated for the last 3500 years and succeeded to an impressive extent in inculcating in the Jewish people. It is no coincidence that it was a Reform rabbi, Felix Adler, who founded the ethical-culture movement (1876).

---

*And if the humanist admits that man needs systematic moral discipline, we welcome his adoption of the Jewish attitude.

7. Judaism offers at least four things which humanism lacks for realizing its ethical ideals:

a) **An ethical system.** Judaism contains the most extensive ethical system known to mankind—see Question 2 for a detailed examination of this system. Does humanism have systematic laws on charity binding on all people born to humanist parents (as Judaism has—see Appendix A)? Is there a two hundred page humanist volume on gossiping (as Judaism has—see p. 174)? Is there *any* humanist code of laws geared to implementing its proclaimed ethics? The answer to these questions is no. Humanism has ideals but no legal system of implementation.

b) **Ethics based on God.** Judaism does not *suggest* to its adherents that they act kindly to fellow human beings, honestly in business, or with compassion to animals; it *commands* Jews in the name of a Being infinitely higher than themselves or their leaders to do so. "Love thy neighbor as thyself, I am God" (*Leviticus* 19:18).

c) **A religious-ethical code.** Since Judaism has the above two things, systematically codified ethics and a transcendent base, Jews have a binding source of morality by which to judge and correct themselves and other Jews. They therefore have a method to ethically improve their fellow Jews—they can say "you have violated such and such a law and God's will." Should a humanist perpetrate evil, what can we say to him—"human experience, reason, the editor of *the Humanist* suggest that you act differently?" In order to improve the ethical behavior of religious Jews we can appeal to the Torah. Should we wish to raise the level of ethical behavior of non-believing persons, to what generally recognized code of binding ethics can we appeal?

d) **A method of transmitting ethics.** For over three thousand years Judaism has transmitted its ethics from generation to generation through study of Judaism and observance of Jewish laws, all of which serve to perpetuate its ethical ideals. What is the system by which ethical ideals are transmitted from the humanist parent to his child? Is not humanism at a distinct disadvantage because it lacks such a system?

CONCLUSION

The crucial question, as posed earlier, is this: which movement is more capable of and more likely to create ethical individuals, ethical humanism or ethical monotheism, humanist ideals or Judaic practices and ideals, well-intentioned individuals or a religiously motivated nation?

Question 5

WHAT IS THE JEWISH ROLE
IN THE WORLD?

In its strong hold over human minds and hearts, uniquely combining religious universalism with individualism and nationalism, lay Judaism's strength and the secret of its future world-transforming career.
William H. McNeill, *The Rise of the West*

The Egyptian, the Babylonian, and the Persian rose, filled the planet with sound and splendor, then faded to dreamstuff and passed away; the Greek and the Roman followed, and made a vast noise, and they are gone; other peoples have sprung up and held their torch high for a time, but it burned out, and they sit in twilight now or have vanished. The Jew saw them all, beat them all, and is now what he always was, exhibiting no decadence, no infirmities of age, no weakening of his parts, no slowing of his energies, no dulling of his alert and aggressive mind. All things are mortal but the Jew: all other forces pass, but he remains. What is the secret of his immortality?
Mark Twain, *Harper's Magazine*, September, 1899

Perfect the World Under the Rule of God

The Jews introduced God into the world, and with God the call to all mankind to live by one moral standard in brotherhood. Each of these revelations—God, one moral law, human brotherhood—was made for the first time 3200 years ago to a few hundred thousand ex-slaves in the Sinai desert. Why this particular group of men and women, at that particular time, should have taken upon themselves and upon all their succeeding generations the task to "perfect the world under the rule of God"* is a mystery which perhaps only the religious can hope to solve. Historically, psychologically, and anthropologically, both the God which that group of Jewish slaves revealed and the task of perfecting the world which they assumed had no precedent in human history.**

"The idea," Professor of Comparative Literature George Steiner of Cambridge University has written, "of an invisible, unspeakable, unpronounceable God, *is perfectly unique. It happened once and once only*, so far as we know, and it is a maddening and crazy idea if you try to take it at all seriously." It ran completely against "the human instinct that rocks and trees and flowers and rivers and sky and stars are divine . . ." (*Psychology Today*, February 1973).

---

*These words, over two thousand years old, are contained in the second paragraph of the *Aleinu* prayer, which is recited three times daily by observant Jews. See the discussion of this prayer in Joseph Hertz's *The Authorized Daily Prayer Book* (New York: Bloch Publishing Company, 1948), pp. 208-211.

**". . . Israelite religion was an original creation. . . . It was absolutely different from anything the pagan world ever knew; its monotheistic world view had no antecedents in paganism"—Professor Yehezkel Kaufmann, *The Religion of Israel* (University of Chicago: 1960, p. 2).

Whether one believes that Moses the "charismatic genius" or some other natural phenomenon is responsible, or that only a divine revelation can explain what occured at Sinai, the fact is that this people did take upon itself to change the world. No matter how intense the suffering— and no people has had to endure the continuous slaughter and torture which the Jews have—this tiny people has persisted in what it never ceased to believe was its divinely appointed role to bring all mankind to the recognition of God and His one moral standard.

It is in this sense of a moral commitment to perfect themselves and the world that the Jews considered themselves "chosen." This consideration never meant advantages for the Jews, only increased responsibilities and hardships. If God did not choose this group of non-entities to provide a moral model society to others, if in fact no divine-human encounter took place at Sinai, we can only conclude that this willingness of a nation to create and to take upon itself such a moral responsibility and burdensome way of life as Judaism (and Jewish sources do refer to it as *ole*, a burden) constitutes the most spectacularly impressive national achievement in human history. If the responsibility of "chosenness" has been a 3200-year-old delusion, we only wish that all nations would have so deluded themselves into self-sacrifice for noble ideals, that all nations would delude themselves into a commitment to observe hundreds of ethical laws requiring self-discipline, and that all nations would judge others by their ethics rather than their religious beliefs.

Despite every conceivable obstacle, many of which no nation has ever survived (such as the loss of a homeland, dispersal throughout the world, and attempted genocide against it), the Jewish people has not only persevered, but precisely because of its chosen task, has succeeded in pursuing what the world-noted University of Chicago histo-

rian, William H. McNeill, calls the Jews' "world-transforming career" (*The Rise of The West*, Chicago: 1963, p.
166).

"It was Judaism," writes the Rev. Edward H. Flannery of
the National Conference of Catholic Bishops, "that brought
the concept of a God-given universal moral law into the
world;" willingly or not "the Jew carries the burden of God
in history [and] for this he has never been forgiven" (*New
York Times*, November 30, 1974). For the world to which
the Jews introduced God and their new ideals of morality,
justice, love, peace, and individual responsibility, was not
then, nor has it ever been, appreciative. Such ideals have
generally been alien and threatening to the prevailing
order. Judaism said that God was higher than all false gods,
all leaders, and all armies; that morality was one and universal, not relative to individuals, nations, or economics;
that love was to be directed to one's neighbor and even to
the stranger (*Leviticus* 19:34), not only to one's self and
family. Judaism gave a vision that "nation shall not lift
sword against nation" to a world in which war and warriors
rather than peace and prophets were glorified; and Judaism
said that every person is ultimately responsible not to the
powerful, but to the Almighty. It is little wonder then, why
hatred of the Jew developed and ultimately became, as
Father Flannery wrote, "the greatest hatred in human history."

Yet despite all physical opposition, Judaism's ideals continued to spread even as mighty empires were crumbling.
And twelve hundred years after Sinai, a group of Jews led
by Paul of Tarsus, seeing the Roman Empire's religion
failing, felt the time ripe to bring the world to "the rule of
God" without, however, the need to first "perfect the
world." Without Halakhah, the Jewish laws aimed at this
perfection, and with God made visible and human, Paul
reasoned, the world will come to Godly perfection. But the

world did not come to Godly perfection, though much of it did eventually come to accept Paul's new religion, Christianity, the first major offshoot of Judaism.

Some 600 years after Paul, in another pagan part of the world where Judaism's ideals had begun to infiltrate,* Muhammad revealed God to the Arabs, and soon the second major offshoot of Judaism, Islam, was born.

The two new religions missionized aggressively and, as a consequence, the Jewish ideal made its way from central Asia through Europe to the New World. But its journey was a hazardous one which did not leave the ideal intact, for Christianity, in particular, increasingly emphasized the rule of God (faith) over the perfection of this world. And partly in reaction to this deemphasis on social action, a third, secular, offshoot of the Judaic ideal was founded by a grandson of two Orthodox rabbis, Karl Marx. This derivative, messianic socialism, or secular messianism, stressed only the perfection of this world, and restructured the Judaic ideal to read: perfect the world under the rule of man.

All the while, however, resentment against the Jew was building up among both those being subjugated to the Jewish offshoots and among followers of the offshoots themselves. Regarding the first, Professor Steiner writes, "the triple Jewish summons to perfection [Jewish ethical monotheism; Christianity and Islam; messianic socialism] built up [against the Jews] murderous resentments in the social subconscious. It made the Jew the 'bad conscience' of

---

*"With Judaism [Muhammad's] acquaintance is intimate and many sided. He learned his lessons well; and when a thorough-going comparison is made of the Koranic material, of all sorts, with the standard Hebrew-Jewish writings then current, we must say with emphasis that his authorities, whoever they were, were men versed in the Bible, in the oral law (Talmud) and the aggada" (Charles C. Torrey, *The Jewish Foundation of Islam*, New York: 1933, p. 61).

Western history." As for the followers of the Jewish derivatives themselves, there was a constant resentment
against the Jew for not joining their particular summons to
perfection; by refusing to acknowledge the movements' au-
thenticity and remaining true to the original Jewish role,
the Jews constituted the 'bad conscience' of these Jewish
derivatives as well. Thus, the Church from the New Testament through the modern period, never quite able to
reconcile itself to the fact that the very people to whom
Jesus appealed were the ones who found his appeal most
wanting, depicted the Jews as "sons of the devil" (e.g.,
John 8:44), and treated these people as befits devils. *

---

*The medieval depiction of the Jews as devils is well documented in
Joshua Trachtenberg's *The Devil and the Jews* (Yale University Press:
1941; also in paperback). Much Church legislation against the Jews was
utilized by the Nazis in formulating anti-semitic legislation. The 3rd
Synod of Orleans in 538 legislated that Jews were not permitted to show
themselves in the streets during Passion Week; a Nazi decree of December 3, 1938 authorized local authorities to bar Jews from the streets on
certain days. The Trulanic Synod ruled in 692 (a ruling reconfirmed
many times by Church leaders) that Christians were not permitted to be
treated by Jewish physicians; on July 25, 1938, the Nazis decreed the
same. Starting with the 12th Synod of Toledo in 681 the Church on at
least fifteen occasions burned the Talmud and other Jewish books, a
practice later common in Nazi Germany. The 4th Lateran Council in
1215, Canon 68, decreed that Jews must mark their clothes with a
badge; on September 1, 1941, the Nazis ruled the same. The Synod of
Breslau in 1267 confined the Jewish community to compulsory ghettos,
and starting in the sixteenth century the Church helped enforce Jewish
ghettoization throughout Europe; on September 21, 1939, Heydrich
issued the Nazi order confining the Jews to ghettos. The Council of Basel
in 1434, at Session XIX, ruled that Jews were not permitted to obtain
academic degrees; on April 25, 1933, the Nazis passed the Law against
Overcrowding of German Schools and Universities. Professor Raul Hil-
berg, who compiled this list, noted that the Germans could move so
efficiently against the Jews because "German bureaucrats could dip into
a vast reservoir of administrative experience, a reservoir which church
and state had filled in fifteen hundred years of destructive activity" (*The
Destruction of the European Jews*, Chicago: 1961 pp. 4-6).

And Muhammad, infuriated by the Jews' rejection of his claims to prophecy, changed the object of Muslim prayers from Jerusalem to Mecca, and expelled the Jewish community of Medina. Although historically less barbaric toward the Jews than the Church, Islam to this day resents the Jews and their rejection of Muhammad who, after all, based his Holy Quran on the Jews' Bible and religion.*

So too, Marx could envision no emancipation for the proletariat until society was emancipated from Judaism, i.e., until the Jews ceased being Jews and assimilated into the working class. To this day, almost the only tenet which virtually every Marxist, Leninist, Trotskyite, and Maoist movement shares is the need for the disappearance of the Jews as a distinct entity. They consider every national liberation movement "progressive" except that of the Jewish people, Zionism, which they label "reactionary" (even when it is composed of Jewish socialists and workers).

Thus, the derivatives of Judaism always welcomed, indeed sought, the Jews' participation in each of their attempts to "perfect the world," though of course such participation had to be as members of the derivative movement. Jews who would accept conversion to Christianity, Islam, or Marxism were assured a good life, free of the sufferings which would accrue to them by remaining Jews. Contrary to one prevalent myth, the fact is that had the Jews converted to any of these majority religions they could have assimilated—indeed a significant percentage of Jews has always assimilated. Why then did the Jews not take the easy way out? Why have Jews felt so committed to surviving?

A significant part of the answer lies in the mission which Jews have never forgotten, the mission which they have

---

*See Abraham Katsh's *Judaism and the Koran* (New York: 1962) for an extensive analysis of the Jewish basis of the Quran.

ceaselessly maintained was given to them by God: to serve, in the ancient words of the Prophet Isaiah, as "a light unto the nations." Today, the Jews are still obligated to press on with their mission to perfect the world under the rule of God. For though Judaism considers Christianity and Islam superior to the pagan religions which they replaced, the two daughter religions compromised on at least three basic tenets of Judaism: First, they emphasized faith (and in the case of Islam, predestination) over this-worldly action; second, they converted hundreds of millions of people by virtue of their physical power rather than by serving as a moral model—and as a result they converted many more bodies than minds; and third, by converting so many people en masse, both religions (not to mention the original Judaic role) were diluted by pagan customs and beliefs.

The Jewish role therefore remains as uniquely revolutionary and urgent as ever. But despite their differences, Judaism, Christianity, and Islam must work together in struggling against the third derivative of Judaism which negates the fundamental element which the three religions do share—God. For we are living during the greatest ideological battle in human history: the ultimate battle between Moses and Marx, between the belief that God is the ultimate reality and the belief that matter is the only reality.

Whether mankind accepts Moses' position that God is the highest being and that morality transcends man or Marx's position that man is god and that no morality transcends him, will decide the future of the human race. If, as Judaism posits, each person is created in the image of God, human life is sacred; but if, as Marxism posits, we are created in the image of matter, then we are only matter. And if we are but matter, the Nazi practice of making Jews into lampshades and bars of soap may be understood as a possible and logical outgrowth of such a view. Matter is not holy, nor does it possess moral categories, and all the Nazis did was rearrange the form of matter from human into inanimate.

When God is declared dead, man dies as a value, and shortly thereafter he dies physically as well. Less than 65 years after Nietzsche announced that for Western man God was dead, the two ideologies based on God's death, Nazism and Communism, built mass extermination camps.

That Marxist materialism with its moral relativism is on the ascendant after the horrors of Hitler and Stalin only serves to reconfirm the fact that people do not choose to learn anything moral from history and to confirm the fact that the Jewish role is confronting its greatest challenge in 3200 years. But let no one prejudge the outcome of this battle on the basis of physical might alone, for Judaism has proven to be the most powerful idea in history.

For the last two thousand years Judaism has had to look inward. It is now time for Judaism to look out into the world and to offer itself as an alternative to utter chaos; and it is time for the world to look into Judaism.

We have learned from the Christian experience that faith in God alone will not produce a moral world; from Marxism and Communism that faith in man alone will not produce such a world; and from the intellectuals and humanists that faith in reason alone will not achieve moral results. There remains Judaism, the creator of the ideal of perfecting the world, the originator of universal ideals and equality—and a system which combines in equal measures reliance upon God, man, and reason.

If all the fourteen million Jews lived by Judaism's values and means, the effect upon a world searching for meaning would be incalculable. If tens of thousands of Jewish professors affirmed that man was created in the image of God, if they lived lives consistent with Jewish ethical imperatives rather than lives which deny the religious reality of the universe and which suppress any identification with the system which gave the world the ethics which they at least preach; if every Jew conducted his or her life in accordance with the Jewish role to perfect the world under the rule of God, the impact upon all of society would be staggering. A moral revolution of unprecedented proportions would be in the making.

We have for the first time in nearly 2,000 years the opportunity to create our model state in Israel. Thus, now nationally, as well as individually, the Jewish people have the capacity to show the world the moral power of the Jewish ideal.

We are living in the age of the death of man; in an age increasingly bored with the good, the holy, and the peaceful. Visceral excitement like sex and violence is becoming the one common denominator of all classes and individuals. An affirmation of something higher is, therefore, called for; and Judaism is the alternative which has proved its moral efficacy over the last 3200 years.

In accordance with Judaism's 3,200 years old directive (*Leviticus* 19:2), an army of tender, caring, strong, moral people must be formed to combat the hordes of bored aimless people and the totalitarian and nihilistic ideologies to which they are prey. The offshoots of Judaism—Christianity, Islam, Marxism, Humanism—now virtually dominate the world. Consciously or not the world has affirmed the goals of Judaism; but it has altered its means. It is time—if there is time—to proceed with the world-transforming event which began 3200 years ago at a mountain in Sinai—the Jewish revolution.

Question 6

WHY ARE SO MANY
YOUNG JEWS ALIENATED
FROM THE JEWISH COMMUNITY?

WHAT ACTIONS CAN WE AS PARENTS
TAKE TO LESSEN THE CHANCES OF
OUR CHILD INTERMARRYING?

Many Jewish parents claim . . . that they gave their children everything that they did not have as children. The problem is, however, that the parents did not give what they did have as children—a basically religious environment.

When you ask your child to refrain from marrying a non-Jew you are making a life-changing demand. The only way such a request will make an impression is if you back it up with life-changing action on your part. It is unfair (and futile) to ask your child to change his or her life if you are not willing to change your own.

Next to the survival of Israel the issue which weighs heaviest upon the American Jewish mind is the loss of Jewish identity among many young Jews. "How can we bring our youth back?" is probably the most oft-posed question in American Jewish life: study groups, symposia, commissions, and the like are constantly being organized to come up with answers to this question. Yet too often we attempt to "bring them back" without understanding why young Jews have left, or, (even more importantly, as we believe) why they were never really with us. We must first understand, therefore, what has caused the alienation of many youth from the Jewish religion and community.

The essential problem underlying this rejection of Jewish identity can be summarized in a single sentence. **For the great majority of young Jews who abandon Jewish identity, it is not Judaism but a caricature of Judaism that they are rejecting.**

The Caricature

Instead of portraying Judaism as the all-encompassing value system and way of life which it is, most Jewish parents and institutions have been treating Judaism as if it were a pastime, something to which one devotes some time, some effort, and some resources, but surely not most of one's time, efforts or resources. Judaism is portrayed as an adjunct to the other, really important, things in one's life. Most parents, consciously or not, express considerably more fear that their children will become "too Jewish" than that they will become too secular, thereby conveying an attitude towards Judaism which can be illustrated in a variety of ways.

THE GREATER IMPORTANCE OF
SECULAR PROFESSIONS

Let us, for example, visit a typical Jewish home on the day when the promising young college junior or senior announces what profession he or she has chosen to pursue upon graduation. The proud Jewish parents are undoubtedly waiting to hear whether their child has picked law, or medicine, or architecture, or any of the numerous other "respectable" fields which so many of our young Jews enter. But, alas, in this particular home, the young Jew reveals that he wishes to enter the rabbinate or some other Jewish profession. After the parents recuperate from their shock, they will probably protest loud and long against this decision which contradicts values they have been reinforcing during their careers as parents: viz., *what type of profession their child enters is of far greater significance than what type of Jew he becomes.* And because Jewish parents have been far more interested in producing accomplished professionals than dedicated Jews, the Jewish community suffers from a surfeit of accomplished professionals who are unaccomplished Jews. The irony is that later in life, many of these parents are saddened by the product which they so diligently molded. How often we hear parents speak of their "wonderful son the lawyer, doctor, or professor" only to add softly "who doesn't care about being Jewish." The choice of a profession is, however, only one of the areas in which young Jews are taught that Judaism is of secondary importance. Judaism also takes second place to secular values and secular education.

THE GREATER IMPORTANCE OF
SECULAR VALUES

Another reason young Jews become convinced that Judaism is of little consequence is that their parents hold an attitude which may be called pseudo-universalism. This view posits that in truth there exists no moral truth* and that since all ethical/religious systems are more or less of equal value (or, perhaps more accurately, of no value), far be it from us Jews to smack of provincialism by raising our children in "too Jewish" an educational and home environment. We dare not "close" our children's minds, but rather we must "open" them to all of mankind's philosophies so that they may—at age thirteen!—freely choose the lifestyle best suited to themselves. Thus, Jewish parents encourage their little children to acquaint themselves with various religious/ethical systems.

The fallaciousness of this all-too-common approach can be shown in two ways. The first can be illustrated with a musical analogy. Suppose a parent who desires to raise a musically accomplished child were to have the child taught to play the piano, violin, oboe, flute, cello, drums, and saxophone. We would consider such an approach absurd, for not only will the child fail to play all those instruments well, he will not be able to play even one of them well. We readily appreciate the fact that in order to become a virtuoso on a musical instrument, a child must concentrate

---

*At a JCY (Jewish Center Youth) weekend in Pennsylvania in November 1974, the fact that most American Jewish youth are raised to believe that there is no moral truth was well illustrated. At one of the sessions which I (D.P.) led, a fifteen year old girl argued that a) Hitler could not be called evil since he believed he was doing good, and "who are we to say who is evil?" and b) even if he was evil, "anyone who would have killed Hitler would have been as evil as Hitler since to kill is wrong." The forty high school students at this session were asked to raise their hands if they agreed with the girl's remarks. All but four raised their hands. Obviously, the fundamental Jewish notion of one God and one moral law (see Question 1) was utterly alien to the thinking of these, and probably most, Jewish youth.

primarily on one instrument; and later, once he is proficient on it, he will be prepared to study and appreciate other instruments.

Unfortunately, most parents have failed to recognize the validity of this principle in relation to religion and ethics. On what basis could a child who is exposed to many differing systems of ethics possibly be expected to make an intelligent choice? By what standard can he measure differing religio-ethical concepts?

When raised by parents who advocate pseudo-universalism a child has no standard by which to judge various lifestyles. Only when a child has standards can he freely choose what lifestyle he ultimately desires—and we would emphasize that later study of other religious/ethical systems and social relations with people of other faiths and nationalities should be encouraged. We suggest this rule: first, "know thyself" as a Jew; and then, remember that "he is wise who learns from every man" (*Talmud*).*

Precisely because young Jews are usually raised in homes which communicate few clear-cut standards—other than the respect of everyone else's standards—and no distinctly Jewish standards, do so many young Jews flounder today in mid-air, prey to any (or no) ideology which catches their imagination.

---

*This willingness to study other systems does not represent a departure from Jewish tradition. Maimonides gratefully acknowledged his debt to Aristotle, while Bahya Ibn Pakudah (whose medieval *Hovot ha-Levovot, Duties of the Heart*, is still studied in Yeshivot throughout the world) not only relied extensively on Sufi Muslim teachers but vigorously defended his right to use Gentiles as teachers of religion and referred to them as *hasidim* 'pious men' (end of the Introduction to his book). Today as well, Rabbi Joseph Baer Soloveichik, perhaps the greatest living Talmudist in the world, acknowledges the influence of Soren Kierkegaard, the nineteeth century Protestant theologian, on his own thought.

A second more obvious analogy further illustrates our point. In other crucial areas of their child's development, do parents present the child with a multiplicity of choices? Do they ask their children: "Do you want to brush your teeth, or would you prefer not to?" "Do you wish to attend school, or would you rather stay at home?"

In any of these areas of life we would consider the offering of choices to children absurd, but in the words of Norman Lamm, ". . . a way of life that will determine whether existence has meaning, whether (the child) is rooted in history or not, whether morality is binding, whether hope and destiny are real or illusions—this any child may choose for himself." (*The Royal Reach*, New York: 1970, p. 310).

THE GREATER IMPORTANCE OF
SECULAR EDUCATION

Secular values are further reinforced by the manner in which we educate Jewish youth. By relegating Jewish education to a few hours per week for a few years (usually until bar-mitzvah, precisely the age when a child can first begin to intellectually appreciate Judaism), we are telling our children ever so eloquently that we deem math, grammar, and social studies—any of which is studied more hours per week than Judaism—of far greater significance than Jewish history, philosophy, religion, and ethics. Furthermore, the unimportance of Judaism implied by the small quantity of Jewish study is confirmed by the generally low quality of Jewish education.

Most young Jews are given a Jewish education equivalent to between a third and eighth grade level, and then are expected to compare Judaism favorably with high school and later university level secular humanism, Marxism, or other philosophical systems (the current vogue being neo-liberal moral relativism and/or detached academicism).

Just as a poor education in chemistry will produce poor chemists or no chemists, so a poor Jewish education will produce poor Jews or no Jews; and the chances of alienation from Jewish identity increase even more in the proportion that secular education surpasses in time and quality Jewish education. *

Alienation From Strongly Jewish Homes

Much less common but even sadder than the alienation of Jewish children who come from Jewishly inactive homes is the alienation of children raised in Jewishly motivated homes. Of these there are two major types: a) homes committed to Jewish causes but not observant of Jewish law and b) homes which are observant of Jewish law.

TYPE A

Many Jewish parents assume that their own deep attachments to the Jewish people and Jewish causes should suffice to insure that their children will retain a strong Jewish identity. Thus one often hears parents lament something like this: "We can't understand how our child could intermarry (or follow a guru . . . or join up with radical—sometimes even anti-Israel—political groups . . . or care so little about being a Jew . . .); we gave so much to the U.J.A. (or devoted so much time to Hadassah . . . or have such strong Jewish feelings . . .)."

---

*A personal note: We did not acquire our fluency in Hebrew and familiarity with Jewish sources from attending Jewish classes for a few hours a week. Until the age of seventeen, we attended the Yeshiva of Flatbush, where we studied Jewish sources—for three to four hours a day (and we might add that this in no way stunted our social and professional development).

Unfortunately, little can be said to these parents. It is extremely difficult to undo the mistakes which parents have wittingly or unwittingly made for twenty years. But in order to help prevent repetition of such problems, it is important to try to understand where these parents went wrong.

At the outset, let us acknowledge one fact unequivocally. To insure the Jewish identity of one's children, it is not *enough* to work diligently for a Jewish organization, contribute to Jewish causes, cry at Jewish tragedies, or possess a "Jewish heart." For while these aspects of Jewish life are noble and *just as essential to Jewish survival* as is the observance of Jewish law, they do not suffice in implanting Jewish identity in one's children.

One reason for this insufficiency is that children often do not perceive communal service as emanating from a particularly deep and sincere commitment to Jewish life, but rather as emanating from some professional, personal, social, or other need. Moreover, even when this work does in fact spring from a deep Jewish commitment, it may have little meaning for the child. For if the parents' entire Jewish identity is at the Federation office or at the Hadassah luncheon, what does the child experience Jewishly himself, at home? What distinctly Jewish values have these parents conveyed to their children? While becoming expert at *how* the Jewish people can survive, few of these parents gave thought to the basic question their children were posing: *why* should the Jews survive?

At the root of this problem lies yet another. Many Jewish parents claim, half in pride and half in sorrow, that they gave their children everything that they did not have as children. The problem is, however, that the parents did not give what they did have as children—a basically religious environment.

The great majority of Jewish parents who work for or

contribute to Jewish causes out of a deep Jewish feeling acquired that feeling by being raised in a more or less religious environment. Had they given more thought to it, these parents would have realized the necessity of creating such an environment for their own children.

As a result of the materially insecure existence of their youth, many Jewish parents concentrated on providing only for the material needs of themselves and their children. As we know now, however, affluence breeds at least as many problems as it solves. When people do not have to worry about their next meal or a roof over their heads, they have time to worry about themselves and about such abstract questions as "What is the meaning of my life?" Our generation can well appreciate the Biblical observation that "not by bread alone shall man live." We are the most affluent generation in human history—and quite possibly the most neurotic since we cannot find meaning in life. Once the needs for food and companionship are fulfilled, the greatest human craving is for meaning.

Thus, instead of diminishing the need for a meaningful and spiritual way of life, affluence and modern technology have immeasurably increased it. The sad spectacle of youths from affluent homes who are utterly lost and prey to peddlers of pseudo-spirituality (e.g., gurus, counter-culture hippies, Krishna devotees, Jesus freaks, et al.) or misguided idealism (e.g., "revolutionary" and "underground" movements) confirms this fact.

TYPE B

Though less frequent, alienation of children from observant homes is not uncommon. Only rarely, however, does alienation from observant homes culminate in total abandonment of Jewish identity; more often it means an abandonment of Jewish observance. The child's alienation stems from an emotional and/or a rational rejection of

Judaism. The former does not come under our present topic of discussion as it is more of a psychological and emotional problem than a religious one. Rejection of the religious beliefs and practices of one's parents is often but one part of a larger rejection of parental influence or one manifestation of a general rebellion against the home.

We must, however, consider the rational religious reasons for a child's rejection of his or her parents' observance. There are children from observant homes who come to view their parents' religious observance as little more than meaningless rituals based upon blind belief. While it is true that some children are content to continue religious practice out of habit, others who are blessed (or cursed) with intellectual curiosity will, as soon as they are exposed to the non-observant world, begin to radically question the religion of their upbringing; and they may eventually conclude that their parents' religion consists of habits which are no more worthy of perpetuation than their parents' other 'personal' habits.

It is essential, therefore, for observant Jewish parents to fulfill at least two requirements in order to insure that their children will continue to be observant. First, they must exemplify the ideals which Jewish law seeks to realize. Observant parents must be able to show that Jewish practice raises their level of idealism and ethics above the average person's: otherwise their children may regard their observance, and thus Judaism in general, as irrelevant, or even a barrier, to a moral or meaningful life.

Second, observant parents must be prepared to offer reasoned and meaningful answers to their children's questions. Certainly once a child reaches his teens, it is not enough to answer questions with "because that's what the Torah says." There are answers to the questions which young Jews ask, and it is the responsibility of every concerned parent to learn those answers.

We are living in a free society, in a huge marketplace of ideas. American Jewish young people are free to choose from among the many ways of life and ideals offered to them. We believe that Jews should deeply welcome this development, for Judaism is the most powerful idea in history (see Question 5) as well as a beautiful way of life. Until a great many more Jews, young and old, share this appreciation, however, the problem of alienation will continue to be a crippling one.

A Note To Parents Concerning Intermarriage

A prominent rabbi told us recently that he had been called about three hundred times in the last decade by frantic parents imploring him to break up the impending intermarriage of their son or daughter. He agreed every time to meet the child, yet he succeeded exactly once in dissuading the person from marrying the non-Jew.

This negligible rate of success may prompt one to dismiss this rabbi as lacking powers of persuasion. Yet, this man, Steven Riskin, is considered by many to be one of the most dynamic and persuasive figures in Jewish life today. The number of young Jews he has attracted to Judaism is staggering. How then does one account for his inability to break up prospective intermarriages?

The answer, sadly, is simple. Parents who approach a rabbi concerning the imminent intermarriage of their child are usually showing serious interest in their child's Judaism about twenty years too late. By this time the child is already in love with a non-Jew, and the only obstacle to the child's complete happiness may be a guilty feeling that if he or she intermarries, "my parents would be distraught." But this will not ultimately affect their decision to intermarry because they will quite logically refuse to sacrifice real feelings of love for vague feelings of guilt.

In most cases, the parents' approach to the rabbi, and their other efforts to prevent their child's intermarriage, constitute the first time that they have ever shown serious interest in Jewish identity. Consequently, it appears to the child quite odd that all of a sudden, Judaism, which until now was treated as a pastime, has become the parents' greatest passion. Had these parents shown a fraction of this Jewish passion during the previous twenty years, however, the child may well have been duly impressed and therefore an unlikely candidate for intermarriage.

Though numerous studies have confirmed the fact, one need not be a sociologist to recognize that intermarriage is rendered far more likely in homes which communicated the caricatured Judaism described in the first part of this answer than in homes which lived an active Judaism. Of course, one can point to the exceptional cases wherein children of actively Jewish homes have intermarried, but such pointing has no point. One can also point to instances wherein seat belts failed to save the lives of passengers in automobile accidents, but just as these instances do not negate the fact that seat belts save lives, so the former exceptions do not negate the fact that actively Jewish homes save Jews.

Children from homes which communicated by words and deeds that Judaism has distinctive values worthy of perpetuation are unlikely to intermarry simply because they are unlikely to find non-Jews (or, for that matter, many Jews) who share their values. If they should happen to find such a non-Jew, this is no problem either, since Jewish conversion enables non-Jews to integrate into Jewish life; and then it is of course not an intermarriage but the marriage of one Jew to another.

The issue of intermarriage also reveals an interesting irony in Jewish life. When asked to characterize the observant Jewish community, non-observant Jews will often refer to the former as "provincial," "closed-minded," and "too Jewish." Yet it would be most instructive to ascertain what arguments against intermarriage these two types of Jews can offer their children. The non-observant "universalist" is compelled to use family or ethnic arguments—true parochialism, whereas the observant "parochialist" can offer arguments ("does he or she share your values?") which appeal to idealism rather than ethnicity.*

The arguments against intermarriage of the less committed Jews are often ultimately rooted in the expressed or unexpressed opinion that Jews are superior (otherwise why not intermarry since there is nothing distinctive about Judaism?). Yet no seriously committed Jew should argue that Jews are inherently superior, simply because he has no reason to think they are. He contends rather that it is Judaism which is a superior system for generating better people, and only insofar as one inculcates this system is he or she more likely to be a moral person. Thus, whereas the traditionalist can use logical arguments to appeal to a young person to perpetuate ties rooted in ideals, other Jews can only make an emotional appeal to perpetuate ties rooted in blood.

Is It Too Late?

At the outset, we stated that Jewish concerns which first manifest themselves once a son or daughter is planning to

---

*This is not to say that observant Jews always do utilize arguments based on values, and to the extent that they do not, they are guilty of the same provincialism as the ethnic Jews.

marry a non-Jew are being expressed about twenty years
too late. Nevertheless even at this late date it is not too late
for you to begin to study and live Judaism, and to thereby
eventually influence your child. If you are asking your child
to make a life-changing decision, you must be fully prepared to do the same. Otherwise your words will be as
futile as they are (unintentionally) hypocritical.

If your son or daughter is a young person contemplating
intermarriage, it is certainly not too late to attempt to
influence him or her Judaically. Should you immediately
transform your home into a *makom-Torah* (a place of
Torah), where Judaism is studied and practiced (especially
with your child(ren)), your child(ren) may begin to treat
Judaism with greater respect, and the likelihood of intermarriage will have been reduced.

Even if your son or daughter is planning (rather than
merely contemplating) marriage with a non-Jew, and even
if he or she has already intermarried, it may not be too late
to influence him or her—and the non-Jewish spouse—to
look into Judaism as a way of life. But, again, your only
chance to influence anyone depends upon your own commitment. Mature people are open to new ideas, and by and
large Judaism may be characterized as a new idea for most
Jews. Even many non-Jews who are married to Jews would
probably be receptive to studying Jewish philosophy, history, and theology and to begin to experiment with
Judaism as a way of life, if it were presented with sophisti-
cation and warmth. We have both had the pleasure of meeting men and women who have converted to Judaism and
who are among the sparks of their respective Jewish communities. We have also met a large number of people who,
though born Jewish, came to take Judaism seriously only
later in their lives, and then developed into communal
leaders.

Thus, it is never definitely too late. After seeing you

infuse your life with deeper meaning your children may also reassess their priorities and eventually realize the error of raising children without historical rootedness and without a religious-ethical way of life. We cannot, of course, promise any miracles. We can only promise you that if you show no commitment to changing your life, you will be offering little reason to your children to change theirs.

Question 7

WHY SHOULDN'T I INTERMARRY?

DOESN'T JUDAISM BELIEVE IN UNIVERSAL BROTHERHOOD?

In maintaining our ancient struggle on behalf of our ideals and our people, the Jews have answered Hillel's two questions: "If I am not for myself, who will be for me? But if I am only for myself, what am I?" Now you too must answer these questions.

This answer is the hardest for us to write. When we write of the centrality of the Jewish role in the world, the cruciality of the Jewish conception of man and God, or the sublime nature of Shabbat, we must appeal to objective reasoning. But when we write of our opposition to intermarriage, we must overcome your emotions as well as appeal to your intellect.

The rest of this book is our answer to this question. If you have read it thoughtfully, we hope that it may have convinced you of the need to keep Judaism and the Jewish people alive. At the very least, however, it should now be clear to you why we—and millions of others—care deeply if you decide to leave Judaism and us.

THE ISSUE: VALUES, NOT ETHNICITY

Our answer depends entirely on what values you have in common with both us and your prospective mate. Take the concepts which we have just enumerated, for example. Do you feel a commitment to the 3500-year-old Jewish people and its role in transforming the world (see Question 5)? Do you feel a commitment to perpetuating the concept of each human being's infinite worth—the concept of man's creation in the image of God rather than in the coincidental image of soulless molecules (see Question 1)? Do you feel a commitment to the ideal of Shabbat and its unique practices (see Questions 2 and 8)?

If you do feel these commitments, then sharing common concerns and values, it is relatively easy for us to communicate with you on the issue of intermarriage. We have but one question to ask of you: Is the person whom you are considering marrying one who will share these commitments and values? If your answer is yes, marry the

person. Judaism welcomes converts who will further
Jewish ideals through observance of Halakha (Jewish
laws).*

If your answer is no, however, then logic dictates not
only the elimination of this non-Jew as a possible mate, but
the elimination of the majority of Jews as well. Both of us
have been involved in relationships with Jews which were
eventually ended because to these women Judaism was
likely to remain a peripheral concern.

Thus, if you are a committed Jew, we do not have to
explain to you why you ought to marry someone who
shares your Jewish concerns. Unless you subscribe to the
foolish romantic notions that "love conquers all" or that you
can only love one person, it should be obvious to you that
the more values and concerns which you share with your
husband or wife the greater the likelihood of a happy and
successful marriage.

But if Judaism is not a central commitment in your life
and you consider Judaism largely irrelevant or at least not
something for which you are prepared to sacrifice a personal relationship, it is far more difficult for us to communicate with you concerning intermarriage. Perhaps all
we can do is address an appeal to you.

------

*Judaism so values sincere converts that it believes that the Messiah
will be a descendant of one, Ruth. But the conversion of which we are
speaking is a sincere commitment to Judaism, not a *pro forma* gesture
made to alleviate the bad feelings of anxious in-laws. Conversions which
make no demands upon the convert to lead a Jewish life oppose all that
Judaism values. Such conversions render Judaism meaningless and
render the Jewish people no more than an ethnic society. As should be
clear from this book, we welcome converts to Judaism, idealistic people
who assume the universal religious system of Judaism. But a sign-on-
the-dotted-line conversion which demands nothing Jewish of the convert
is not a conversion to Judaism. It is merely a fraudulent solution to the
problem of intermarriage.

We would begin by asking you not to reject a way of life which you do not know. And please do not fool yourself—you really do not know Judaism. The few hours of bar or bat-mitzvah chanting, lulav shaking and spitball shooting which you probably experienced each week at Hebrew School simply cannot enable you to know or to judge Judaism. You may be able to judge the Judaism (or lack of it) of your parents and/or the Judaism of your local temple; but the Judaism which has survived 3500 years, the Judaism which bequeathed to the world God and universal morality, the Judaism which survived Pharaoh, Rome, the Crusades, Chmelnitzky (who murdered one third of the Jewish people in 1648), and Hitler and Stalin, and the Judaism which today puts the Jewish people at the vortex of human affairs, is the authentic and powerful Judaism of which, sadly, you know very little. Concerning the natural and social sciences and the arts you are probably quite knowledgeable, but with regard to Judaism and its concerns about the most fundamental issues of meaning and purpose of existence, you know virtually nothing (or maybe even worse, know only the caricatured Judaism described in the previous chapter).

Therefore we appeal to your mind to begin to study authentic Judaism and Jewish history, and we appeal to your heart to begin experiencing Judaism as the beautiful way of life which it is. Once you have studied and developed intellectually and experientially as a Jew, you are, of course, free to reject Judaism. But we think it fair to say that rejection out of ignorance of a system of the most significant ideas in history is intellectually unjustifiable. And though Judaism, as evidenced throughout this book, is based on ideals and ideas rather than ethnicity, we would add that the rejection of an entire people with its embattled 3500 years of history and its present battle for survival is historically unjustified and ultimately rather selfish.

In the eyes of the rest of the Jewish community, the intermarrying Jew is abandoning ship while committed Jews are fighting to keep it afloat. In addition to perpetuating the ideal of perfecting this world in a world which increasingly evokes cynicism rather than idealism, committed Jews feel a personal commitment to insure that the Jewish people never again suffers a holocaust. Thus we fight on behalf of our brothers and sisters in Israel, the Soviet Union, Syria, and anywhere else where small Jewish numbers invite attacks. In maintaining our ancient struggle on behalf of our ideals and our people the Jews have answered Hillel's two questions: "If I am not for myself, who will be for me? But if I am only for myself, what am I?" Now you too must answer these questions.*

INTERMARRIAGE AND YOU

Consider the following:

If you say that being Jewish has no meaning for you, are you certain that this is really so? What were your reactions, for example, during the three weeks prior to the Six-Day War when it appeared that Israel might be annihilated? What were your reactions on and after Yom Kippur, 1973, when once again the Jewish state was threatened with destruction? Did you follow the news on those days with no greater interest or frequency than usual? Did you

---

* As Herman Wouk has written of Jews who leave the Jewish community: "These people . . . are lost from Judaism, that is all; lost down a road which has swallowed many more Jews than the Hitler terror ever did. Of course they survive as persons. But from the viewpoint of an army, it makes little difference whether a division is exterminated or disperses into the hills and shucks off its uniforms" (*This Is My God*, New York: 1959, p. 256).

feel as personally uninvolved in Israel's situation as your
non-Jewish friends and co-workers most likely did? If
indeed your emotional reactions to these events were in no
way exceptional, perhaps being Jewish really has no meaning for you.

But, if events such as the Nazi holocaust, or the possibility of Jews again being slaughtered en masse (in Israel,
or elsewhere), or the present reality of Jews being tortured
in Syria and persecuted in Russia hits you emotionally
more than it does your non-Jewish friends, chances are that
being Jewish means more, perhaps much more, to you than
you think. And it is eminently possible that in the near
future it will come to mean far more than at present. In
fact, should such a change take place you will be in good
company. Many of the foremost Jewish leaders of the last
two hundred years were people who in their youth could
not care less about being Jewish, and who only later in
their lives came to realize the centrality of Judaism to
themselves and to the world.

Theodore Herzl, the founder of modern Zionism and the
man ultimately most responsible for the creation of Israel,
was an assimilating Hungarian Jew until he discovered how
profoundly Jewish he was during the Dreyfus case in 1894
when he heard French mobs shouting "Death to the Jews."

When Moses Hess, *the man who converted Friedrich
Engels to socialism* and influenced the young Marx, was in
his twenties, he considered Judaism to be irrelevant. Yet
within two decades, this father of socialism broke with
Marx and Engels over the amoral nature of their ideology,
and Moses Hess devoted all his later years to working for
Judaism and the Jewish people. In 1862, he wrote in the
beginning of his book *Rome and Jerusalem:* "Here I stand
once more, *after twenty years of estrangement,* in the midst
of my people; I participate in its holy days of joy and
mourning, its memories and hope, its spiritual struggles in

its own house and with the people among which it lives. . . .
A thought which I had stifled forever within my heart is
again vividly present with me; the thought of my nationality, inseparable from the inheritance of my ancestors, the
Holy Land and the eternal city, *the birthplace of the belief
in the divine unity of life and in the future brotherhood of
all men.* This thought, buried alive, had for years throbbed
in my sealed heart, demanding outlet. But I lacked the
energy necessary for the transition from a path apparently
remote from Judaism as mine was, to that new path which
appeared before me in the hazy distance . . ." (emphases
ours).

Another such Jew was a Russian poet of such extraordinary talent that Maxim Gorki, the father of Soviet literature, predicted that he would become one of the great
Russian writers. Yet, with apparent suddenness, Vladimir
Jabotinsky decided that it was more important to help
fellow Jews establish their own homeland than to devote
his life to poetry.

Had you asked any of these men when they were twenty
years old if being Jewish was of any significance to them,
let alone a reason not to intermarry, they would probably
have ridiculed the question. Yet, within a few years each of
these men discovered something he had not previously
known, that being Jewish was the most important thing in
his life.

INTERMARRIAGE AND YOUR MARRIAGE

Since this change in philosophy of life and identification is
a real possibility, consider how you would feel should you
discover one day when Israel or Jews elsewhere were in
great danger, that while you were deeply troubled, your
spouse, though expressing some concern, did not care

nearly as much as you, or perhaps even at all. Or consider how you would feel if you wanted to give to a Jewish cause and found your spouse objecting to this sudden display of "religion." Or consider how self-conscious you might feel should you one day decide to start reading up on Jewish history or religion. We are not asking you to imagine the impossible, for we have repeatedly come across sad cases (including marriages between two Jews) wherein one spouse begins to feel much more for Judaism and/or the Jewish people than does the other.

This development can become a major source of tension, for once you have incorporated ideals into your life they are not easily lost. Unless you are certain that being a Jew is never likely to be a factor of any significance in your life, it is advisable that you discuss your present and potential Jewishness with your non-Jewish friend or fiancé(e); and in order to forestall a potentially serious source of friction

a) reconsider the desirability of your marrying each other; and/or

b) take time out to know yourself better as a person and as a Jew; and/or

c) introduce your non-Jewish boy or girl friend and yourself to Judaism so as to know how both of you would react to authentic Judaism.

The statistics bear out our observation that marriage is difficult enough without the added problem of differing values and religions. Before you intermarry, dispassionate considerations of potential sources of tension can only help.

INTERMARRIAGE AND YOUR CHILDREN

As a final consideration, we would ask you to recognize the effects which your intermarriage will have upon your children. First, and most obvious, you should be aware that your children are hardly likely to grow up as Jews. This is a fact of contemporary life as reported by the noted sociologist of American Jewry, Marshall Sklare: "Many intermarried parents declare . . . that upon maturity their child will have the right to choose his own identity. This generally means that his identity will be with the majority group. Only if the child has formed a particularly strong identification with the parent who is Jewish will he be motivated to integrate into the minority community. *The majority of the children of intermarried Jews, then, will be Gentiles . . . (America's Jews,* New York: 1971, p. 202, emphasis ours).

Admittedly, the likelihood of your children not growing up as Jews may not particularly disturb you. But there are two other negative effects of intermarriage upon children which should disturb you irrespective of your present feelings regarding Judaism.

No Source From Which To
Receive Moral Guidance

Since neither you nor your future spouse strongly affirms his respective religion and yet neither of you wishes to convert to the other's religion, your children cannot be raised with any religious-ethical system. In order not to offend either spouse, neither Judaism nor Christianity will be practiced authentically; and it is wrong to assume that some innocuous hybrid of the two religions can be constructed so as to communicate the ethics of both. There are significant differences between Judaism and Christianity (see Question 4, Part 1) and the attempt to amalgamate the two will not lead to an amalgamated religion, but to no religion at all. In the words of George Santayana, "to attempt to be religious without practicing a specific religion is as possible as attempting to speak without a specific language."

As we have noted on a number of occasions, *telling one's*

children to be ethical does not suffice to render them ethical; an ethical system based on religious values is needed.*
Yet it is precisely such a system which cannot be transmitted in an intermarriage. Thus, your children will be denied what is, along with love, the single most important thing which a parent must give to a child: a strong moral education and way of life.

From where, if not from a religious system in the home, will your children derive ethical values strong enough to withstand a lifetime of challenges? "What contemporary social institution can be counted on to give Western man a strong sense of moral direction? The university? The mass media? The corporation? The country club? The laboratory? The couch? Today only religious faith . . . can provide the basis for a social ethic worthy of the name . . ." (Eugene Borowitz, *The Condition of Jewish Belief*, New York: 1969, p. 32).**

Existential Loneliness

There is yet another negative effect which your intermarriage will have on your children. You will have effectively cut them off from identification with any community.

---

*The need for an ethical system is discussed in Question 2, and the need for ethics based upon God is discussed in Question 1.

**Unless the home provides a source of firm moral education and guidance a child will learn his values (or non-values) from the street and from television. As discussed in Question 6, a lack of moral education is common in non-intermarried homes as well. But at least if two Jewish parents realize the error of not rearing their children in a religious-ethical system, the only obstacle they will have to overcome is ignorance of Judaism. In an intermarried home the obstacles are only too obvious.

Instead of affirming for yourself and passing on to your children what so many lost and lonely individuals in modern societies desperately seek, a sense of rootedness and kinship with others, you will have utterly cut yourself and your children off from any sense of belonging to anything beyond your immediate family. You are thereby bequeathing to your children the single greatest source of neuroses in the modern world: alienation.

Consider this empirically based observation of C.G. Jung, one of the most prominent psychoanalysts of the twentieth century: "I should like to call attention to the following facts. During the past thirty years people from all civilized countries of the earth have consulted me. I have treated many hundreds of patients, the largest number being Protestants, the smaller number Jews, and [about] five or six believing Catholics. *Among all my patients in the second half of life—that is to say, over thirty-five—there has not been one whose problem in the last resort was not that of finding a religious outlook on life. It is safe to say that every one of them fell ill because he had lost that which the living religions of every age have given to their followers, and none of them has been really healed who did not regain his religious outlook*" (emphasis ours—see *Modern Man in Search of a Soul*, Kegan Paul, London: 1933, p. 264).

When we consider the alternative to this self-imposed alienation, the tragedy of this cutting of Jewish roots is revealed with even greater clarity. Jewish life is communally based (so much so that we possess almost no prayers in the singular first person form) and is structured so as to endow each Jew's life with historical and communal meaning. When the Jewish child is born, it is a major event not only for the immediate family but for the community. When the Jewish boy is circumcised at eight days of age, it is not an antiseptic surgical procedure, but a communal

celebration of the entrance of another Jew into the coven-
ant with God. When the Jewish girl reaches her twelfth
birthday and the Jewish boy his thirteenth, they do not
celebrate it alone or at some party but with the community
as it confirms them as responsible adult members.When
two Jews marry, their wedding is more than just a wedding, it is a communal event sanctified "according to the
laws of Moses and Israel." Should Jews in Israel or elsewhere become targets of hatred and bigotry, the young
Jewish man and woman will join with their community in
order to raise funds, mount political pressure, and do
whatever else may be needed to aid fellow Jews—people
whom they have never seen, whose country they have
probably never visited, and whose native language they
most probably cannot speak. When the committed Jew
travels anywhere in the world—from Morocco to Siberia to
Alexandria, Louisiana (among the many places where we
can personally testify to having been beautifully received
by fellow Jews)—he or she is not alone but will assuredly
find brothers and sisters who will take him in, feed him,
and show him love. Finally, when the Jew dies, the community takes part in this aspect of the Jews' life-cycle as
well. The community ensures a dignified burial, mourns for
this Jew, visits and comforts the relatives who are sitting
shiva (seven days of mourning) and lights yearly candles of
remembrance for him or her.

Man is a social animal, and from the beginning of time
and in all societies men and women have united together to
form communities. Whether or not a person finds meaning
and happiness in life often depends on his sense of kinship
with others. The community of Israel stands ready to share
with all its members its joys and sorrows. They have been
doing that for more than three thousand years. They did it
for your great-grandmother and great-grandfather in
Poland (or Russia, Germany, Syria, etc.) and for your

parents in America. They will not do it for your son or daughter, because you have chosen to remove your son or daughter from the Jewish community.

DOESN'T JUDAISM BELIEVE IN UNIVERSAL BROTHERHOOD?

This question is analogous to asking if Einstein believed in relativity. Judaism discovered and is the source of the ideal of universal brotherhood. The Jewish Prophets are universally acknowledged to have been the earliest and most impassioned advocates of universal peace and brotherhood.

But how are we to achieve universal brotherhood? Is the aimless assimilation of the minority of Jews into majority cultures the answer? No, the answer is shared values.

It is precisely due to our commitment to the human race that we so ardently desire the realization of Judaism's goals. When we ask a Jew to reconsider his or her decision to intermarry, it has nothing whatsoever to do with negative feelings towards non-Jews, or even with automatically positive feelings towards those born as Jews. Our consideration is based on our commitment to the Jewish goal of perfecting the world.

Question 8

HOW DO I START ACTING JEWISH?

1) Introduction
2) Shabbat observance
3) Israel
4) Soviet Jewry
5) Lashon Ha-Rah
6) Blessings, Prayers and Tefillin
7) Tzedaka
8) Learning About Judaism
9) Final Considerations

ON PUTTING THEORIES INTO PRACTICE

There is a well-known story about a rabbi who, upon coming to a new congregation, was taken aside by the president and in a friendly manner advised not to talk about certain topics from the pulpit: Hebrew schools—because the children had to take music and dancing lessons and needed the afternoons for play; the Sabbath—because in America one was compelled to work on the Sabbath to make a living, and making a living came first; the Dietary laws, Kashrut—because it was only an ancient health measure, out of place in modern times and, furthermore, too much trouble for the women to bother with two sets of dishes. The rabbi, surprised at the counsel he was receiving, asked anxiously: "If I cannot talk about Hebrew schools and I cannot talk about the Sabbath and I cannot talk about

Kashrut, what can I talk about?" The president replied in mild astonishment: "Why, that is no problem at all; just talk about Judaism!"

Samuel Dresner, *The Jewish Dietary Laws*

Part 1

INTRODUCTION

The "Not Yet" Approach

When Franz Rosenzweig, one of the leading Jewish thinkers of the twentieth century, was once asked if he put on Tefillin (the phylacteries that Jewish men are supposed to place next to their head and heart each morning), the scholar answered, "Not yet." At that point in his life, Rosenzweig did not feel spiritually ready or comfortable with the idea of putting on *Tefillin*—but he did not believe his unreadiness should, or would, be permanent. By answering "not yet" rather than "no," Rosenzweig made known his intention to continue to grow spiritually. Though he was not yet ready, he foresaw the day when wearing *Tefillin* would be a natural expression of his religious growth.

In order to elevate themselves to the task of perfecting the world, the Jewish people must begin to answer questions about their personal observance with Rosenzweig's "not yet." "Do you follow the Jewish command to give 10% of your earnings to *tzedaka*?" "Not yet, but I am giving a little more of my income each year." "Do you observe the Shabbat in your household in full compliance with Judaism's command to both *remember* and *observe* the Shabbat day to make it holy?" "Not yet fully, but we have started to recite the *Kiddush* (blessing over the wine) and the *Birkat Hamazon* (grace after meals) at our Shabbat meals. We have also been able to liberate our family from reliance upon the television to entertain us, and we will soon be starting a Shabbat discussion group with our friends." "Have you done all that you can for Soviet Jewry?" "Not yet, but the whole family recently participated in a Soviet Jewry demonstration, and we are beginning to correspond with a Russian Jewish family awaiting a visa." "Do you observe the laws of Kashrut?" "Not yet entirely, but we no longer eat pork or shellfish, and we don't mix meat and milk at the same meal."

The true profundity of the "not yet" answer is that it is applicable to the Jew who has tried to observe Judaism for many years as well as to the Jew who has just begun to incorporate Judaism into his or her life. "Do you follow the laws of *tzedaka?*" "Not yet fully. Though I give 10% of my income to *tzedaka* I am not sufficiently involved in insuring that poorer people do not come to need *tzedaka*. But I'm trying. I just made a loan to a family who needed it to avoid a foreclosure on their house." "Do you observe the Shabbat in your household according to Jewish law?" "Not yet fully. True, I and my family do not violate any of the Shabbat laws, but too often still I sleep away most of the day. So I am starting a *chavruta* (learning with a friend) every week after synagogue to make sure that I keep up with my Jewish studies." "Have you done all that you should for Soviet Jewry?" "I have not yet done enough. True, for years I and my family have gone to demonstrations and written letters, but now we're starting a new project. We have now become active in the Student Struggle for Soviet Jewry and the National Conference on Soviet Jewry." "Do you observe the laws of Kashrut?" "We do observe Kashrut but not yet in all its moral ramifications. So we are lending support to groups which protest and fight inhumane trapping, seal clubbing, and other barbaric forms of hunting. Also, since there is in our community a large university where very few of the Jewish students are keeping kosher, either because they do not know the reasons for Kashrut, or because it is too expensive, some friends and I have made it known to the Hillel rabbi and to local Jewish student groups that we have an open home where students are invited for a Shabbat or weekday meal."

If Jews, individually and communally, were to start answering "not yet," it would remind us that in the search for God and righteousness all of us are "not yet" there and that we therefore need each other's help. To paraphrase Jakob Petuchowski, this approach to Judaism will generate unity among all Jews whose pattern of religious observance derives from a like desire to hear God's commandments. The "not yet" approach has inspired one traditional rabbi to write: "When someone who eats in a non-kosher restuarant orders beefsteaks instead of porkchops because he keeps kosher, I can no longer laugh at him. His choice was occasioned by a sort of low-level, yet very genuine, concern not to eat of impure beasts. . . . When he refuses butter on it and milk with his coffee because of 'seethe not the kid in its mother's milk,' I respect him still further. And if he orders a scalebearing fish instead of meat, I see him struggling honestly to do God's will" (Zalman Schachter, in *The Condition of Jewish Belief*, New York: 1969, p. 211).

As you read this section on acting Jewish, bear in mind that we are not setting down imperatives that you must follow, nor do we wish to imply that we have mastered everything we suggest. If asked whether we follow everything we have written here, we too would answer, "Not yet." What we have set down are the activities that we have found help stimulate a dynamic Jewish life. This answer is certainly not meant to outline all of Jewish law in the areas discussed.* It is meant rather to answer the question, "How do I start acting Jewish?"

---

*For the reader who wants practical advice on the observance of Jewish law and the incorporation of Jewish values into his life there are two recently published and excellent books available. The first, *To Be A Jew* by Rabbi Hayim Halevy Donin (New York: Basic Books, 1972), is a guide to Jewish observance in contemporary life. Though Donin is Orthodox, the book has been acclaimed by leading Conservative and Reform figures. In this work Donin sets down in 310 pages Jewish laws in areas ranging from Kashrut and Shabbat observance to charity, slander, and employer-employee relationships. The second book, *The Jewish Catalog* (Philadelphia: Jewish Publication Society, 1973) by Richard Siegel and Sharon and Michael Strassfeld, has become a Jewish best-seller in the United States. The catalog is a uniquely lively and creative guide to Jewish living. In addition to describing how to build a Jewish library, the rudiments of keeping kosher, and how to bring a lively and creative spirit to your Shabbat table, it is probably the one book which also tells you how to make a *shofar* (the ram's horn blown on the New Year) or how to crochet a *kippah* (Jewish headcovering). Both of these books should occupy a prominent place in the house of any family concerned with bringing authentic Jewish traditions and teachings into its household.

Part 2

SHABBAT OBSERVANCE

Rabbi Mendl of Kotzk once said, "I don't want you to sin, not because it is wrong, but because there isn't enough time." I cannot feel that the important issue in nonobservance of the Shabbat is sin, but it certainly is a missed opportunity which can never be recovered. A Shabbat that I miss can never happen to me again. I have lost it.

Rabbi Richard Israel, *The Condition of Jewish Belief*

"All beginnings are difficult" (*Mekhiltah Yitro* 19:5).

The best way to start observing the Shabbat is by reserving every Friday night for a large and lengthy meal. This may not be an easy thing in the beginning, particularly for families with children, but after one or two months you will not be able to imagine a Friday night without the Shabbat meal.

We would suggest the following guidelines for a successful Shabbat:

1. Prepare for it all week.

a) Ask little children to make a Jewish craft or learn a Jewish poem or song to present to the family. Older children might review a Jewish article or book, lead a discussion, etc.

b) Bring out the best tablecloth and silverware and have everyone wear clothing which manifests the fact that the Shabbat is special.

2. Light the Shabbat candles.

3. Bless the children.

This blessing, which is recited after the Kabbalat Shabbat, the Friday night prayer service, is said by parents. The father, or mother, or both, place their lips on the child's forehead and hold the child while reciting to a son "May God make you like Ephraim and Menasheh," and to a daughter "May God make you like Sarah, Rebekah, Rachel and Leah."

Herbert Wiener, an American Reform rabbi, who witnessed an elderly North African Jew reciting such a blessing in Safed, Israel, was moved to write, "I could not help but think of successful suburban fathers who had made comfortable provisions for their children, yet would never receive the honor and respect that had fallen to the lot of the old North African Jew who could offer only blessings" (*9½ Mystics*, New York: 1969, p. 257).

American Jews who have incorporated this custom into their homes have reported some other unexpected dividends. In one household with which we are acquainted the children now reciprocate the parents' blessings with their own.

In another household, neighbors witnessing the ritual asked what gift the parents were planning to purchase for their daughter. They assumed that the parents promised the little girl a gift because her face lit up after her father whispered something to her.

4. Recite the Kiddush.

The Kiddush is usually recited by the head of a household, the father. However, a woman may recite it after him, and in a place where there is no male household head, such as a coed student community, a woman may recite it initially. It is also important to encourage small children to recite the Kiddush so as to train them in Shabbat observance and to give them a feeling of participation.

At the end of the Kiddush, all present respond "amen," the reciter drinks from the cup of wine, and then passes the cup around for all to drink.

The Kiddush stresses two motifs: imitation of God and freedom. On the seventh day we rest in imitation of God who created for six days and rested on the seventh. And on the Shabbat we are free, as we work for no man and are under the yoke only of God.

5. Wash hands before eating the challah.

Though many Jews believe that Judaism ordained the washing of one's hands before meals for hygienic reasons, this belief is wrong. Jewish law demands that one's hands be hygienically clean *before* this ritual washing. The purpose of this washing is spiritual, and it indicates a new beginning. The world was submerged in water, and emerged from water to life; a fetus is submerged in liquid and emerges from liquid to life; a woman and a man dip into a *mikveh* (for ritual immersion) and emerge from submersion in water to a renewed beginning. Likewise, we immerse our hands in water, recite a blessing, and affirm the *spirituality of the meal* of which we are about to partake. This is followed by the cutting and distribution of the challah accompanied by the *hamotzi*, the blessing "Blessed are You, Lord our God, King of the Universe, who brings forth bread from the earth."

6. Sing throughout the meal.

The singing should consist of the traditional Shabbat *Zmirot* or other Hebrew or English songs suitable for the Shabbat atmosphere. One can learn the words and tunes through any of numerous Hebrew records that have been released in the United States and Israel during the last few years.

After hearing everyone singing and seeing the candles

lit and everyone dressed up, a visiting six-year-old girl from a non-observant home exclaimed, "Hey, what's the party for?" "We have such a party *every* Friday night," we all answered. Why didn't she?

7. Recite the *Birkat Hamazon* (*grace at the end of the meal*).

The meal concludes with a thank-you to God, the elaborate grace of the Shabbat meal. This prayer expresses thanks to God for, among other things, providing for our material needs and not forcing us to depend on charity, while it also repudiates preoccupation with material possessions.

8. Study and discuss texts and ideas at the table and afterwards.

According to the Talmud, "The Shabbat and festivals were only given to Israel to provide them with an opportunity to study Torah." It is particularly crucial today, when the Jewish community is by and large Jewishly illiterate, that the Shabbat meal also serve an educational function. No matter what the age of the children, the family should study the weekly portion of the Torah with its commentaries and legendary teachings and attempt to extract the ethical import of the Torah's stories and laws.

The following discussion of the tale of Sodom and Gomorrah is an example of the philosophical and moral profundity to be found in but one Torah chapter:

Genesis 18 narrates the story of Sodom and Gomorrah, two ancient Near Eastern cities inhabited and controlled by evil men. The Bible, in recounting God's decision to destroy these cities, also tells of a unique debate that occurred between Abraham and the Creator. When God informed Abraham of His decision to destroy the cities, Abraham protested and made an appeal. "Shall not the judge of all the world act with justice?" (18:25), protested Abraham, and he appealed to God to save the cities if 50, or 45, or 40, or 30, or 20, or even only 10 righteous people be found within them.

Each time Abraham made his appeal, God did indeed re-examine the cities to see if He could find the requisite number of righteous people. When it became apparent that with the exception of one family the entire populace was evil, God proceeded to destroy the cities.

This chapter is a good example of how the Bible confronts a universal theme—in this case, evil—and outlines its ideals in a manner that makes the study of the Bible meaningful for both children and adults.

Children learn from this story that there are objective moral standards that are applicable and absolutely binding not only when the majority supports them, but even in places like Sodom and Gomorrah (read Nazi Germany and the Soviet Union) where evil is called good, and that evil deserves to be, and ultimately is, punished.

These rather obvious points, however, barely scratch the surface of all that is suggested within the Sodom and Gomorrah story. For thousands of years, Jewish commentators and philosophers, and ordinary Jews at their Shabbat tables, have discussed other implications of this narrative.

a) What is the significance of Abraham's debating with God? Does Abraham's challenge to God have any implications for modern man? Do we too have a right to cry unto God "shall not the judge of all the world act with justice?" And if we do, when does this right apply?

b) A closer reading of the text will also bring us to confront an oft-posed philosophical question: *is an action good because God says so, or does God say it is good because it is good?* This chapter seems to reflect the latter view, for Abraham seems to be saying that God's decision to destroy

Sodom is not just unless God can morally justify this decision. *Genesis* 4:10 also seems to support the notion of a
universal morality inherent in the universe. Though God
had not yet given the Ten Commandments or any other law
prohibiting murder, He still holds Cain to account for murdering his brother Abel, meaning that Cain should have
innately perceived murder to be wrong.

c) Though the two of us have read this story dozens of
times and thought we had exhausted every possible sub-
tlety implicit in the Biblical narrative, we recently studied
this portion with friends—and learned how wrong we were.
We had always assumed that Abraham was pleading for
the righteous men of Sodom and Gomorrah rather than for
the cities themselves. But our friends noted that this is not
what the Bible says. If Abraham's concern was for the
righteous men alone, he would have requested of God that
they be led from the city in safety. But nowhere does he
suggest this. His appeal is that all the people of the cities be
saved should ten righteous men be found within them.

From this analysis of just one chapter of the Bible, it
should be apparent that the study of Jewish sources will
provide material that is intellectually stimulating and morally elevating. It should also be apparent that anyone wishing to create a Shabbat atmosphere which leads to holiness
and moral development must study such material with his
family and friends (and alone) at the Shabbat table, and
with a group of friends at other times on Shabbat.

9. Try to raise the level of your talk to the level of Shabbat.

If you have followed the first eight suggestions, the atmosphere at your Shabbat table should be very different
from, and raised to a much higher level than, the atmosphere at your table the rest of the week. But one thing can
destroy this beautiful atmosphere: gossip. Therefore, *attempt to speak about ideas and issues rather than per-*

sonalities. Should you succeed in doing this, it will not be
long before your Tuesday night meals are uplifted too.

10. **Our final suggestion is an emphatic one:** *No televi-
    sion on Shabbat.*

The purpose of television is to entertain, of Shabbat to
challenge; of television to enable people to kill time, of
Shabbat to teach people how to use and sanctify time; of
television to watch others perform, of Shabbat to make you
perform. According to the Nielsen studies, a television is
on in American households more than six hours a day. By
keeping it off one day each week you will liberate on that
day more than one third of the time the average American
family is awake. The Shabbat challenges you to rely on
your own resources. The Shabbat is a natural day, no artifi-
cial additives are permitted. *Therefore, no television!*

Peace Between You and Your Fellow Man and Woman

The Shabbat experience should be shared with other
people. Thus, if you have a Shabbat meal at your home,
invite others to share your Shabbat. Make a special effort
to have at your table people who, for whatever reason, are
alone on Shabbat. Share your Shabbat with widows and
widowers, divorced and single people, and students. If
there is a family of Soviet Jews in your community, invite
them; they have probably never participated in a traditional Shabbat.

But, of course, reserve time on Shabbat to be alone with
those you love. Let the family rejoice *together* on the Shabbat. It is much more difficult on Wednesday.

Peace Between Man and Nature

The Shabbat aims to create a state of peace between us
and our world. Walk through nature on the Shabbat to
observe and appreciate God's wonders, but do not exploit

that which you see. Don't pick a beautiful flower even if it is to be a gift for someone you love. Confine your giving to a verbal description of what you have seen. Luxuriate in your garden. But do not dig, plant, fertilize, weed, cut, trim, mow or water it. When you reenter your house do not look around for what needs repairing. The Shabbat is not a day for household chores. And, of course, since you should not start a fire (*Exodus* 35:2), do not cook or smoke. *On the Shabbat let nature rest just as you do; let nature be free of domination by man just as you are.*

Peace Between You and God

Take time out for yourself on Shabbat, to think, study, and reflect. Be internally creative. As Rabbi Moses Tendler of Yeshiva University has written: "For six days we share with the beasts of the field a common goal—material sustenance. Only on the Shabbat day when we proclaim God the creator and man as one created in His image do we assume truly human proportion. To rest by lying on a hammock, ruminating on a large meal, would be a further mimicry of the animal world. To rest by spending the day in intellectual disquietude, by mind-wracking study of God and man, by fatiguing examination of the children's studies that week, is a uniquely Jewish concept" (*The Condition of Jewish Belief*, New York: 1969, p. 241).

Conclusion

If you adopt the Shabbat, it will become an experience you will constantly reflect on with pride, an experience which you will increasingly want to share with your friends and your children's friends. We believe that the Shabbat ideal has the inherent potential to transform a strife-torn world into a harmonious, peaceful one, a world preoccupied with amassing material wealth, into one concerned with attaining spiritual greatness.

And remember: the more different you make the Shabbat, the more beautiful it will become.

Part 3

ISRAEL

Only if there are many committed Jews living in Israel will we be able to fulfill the Jewish role in the world, the creation of a Jewish society to serve as a moral model to the world. Therefore, among the best things you can do for yourself, your children and the world is to **make Aliyah,** i.e., **go and live in Israel.**

Should Aliyah prove to be impossible for you at this time, however, we urge you to take the following actions to solidify your ties with the Jewish state.

1. Visit Israel as often as you can. Travel around the country and meet its people. Come to feel at home in Israel. You are.

2. Live for a year in Israel. If you are a student, this is relatively easy to arrange. There are openings at every Israeli university (and at many high schools), at most Yeshivot (most of which are restricted to either men or women), and at kibbutzim (which are in constant need of people who are willing to work hard in exchange for room, board, and classes in Hebrew). If you are an undergraduate, you should seriously consider spending a year in Israel even if it means delaying your B.A. a year. The year will give your life the kind of meaning that no academic degree can.

Spending a year in Israel should not, of course, be confined to students. Everyone, no matter what his or her field of work, should plan to live one year in the one country in the world that has the potential to create a society based on Judaism. You need Israel as much as it needs you.

3. Learn Hebrew. This is a most important way to insure a meaningful visit and/or a comfortable adjustment

to living in Israel. Many Israelis speak English, but
Hebrew is their first language and it is rapidly becoming
the second language of Jews everywhere else. The more
Hebrew you know when you come to Israel, the more of the
country you will appreciate—and the more you will be appreciated.

While you are still here . . .
  1. Learn the issues in the Middle East conflict. There
is always increased support for Israel's right to live in
peace and security when people know the facts of the
Arab-Israeli dispute. See to it, therefore, that your
friends, Jewish and non-Jewish, know the facts and are
able to counter anti-Israel propaganda with the truth. To
start, we strongly recommend reading *Myths and Facts—
1974* published by *Near East Report* (1341 G Street NW,
Washington, D.C. 20005) and available at fifty cents a copy.
It is an excellent presentation of factual responses to Arab
myths about Israel. It is must reading for anyone who
wishes to present the case for Israel.
  2. Reach out to the general American community. It
is imperative that Jewry not confine its pro-Israel lobbying
to Congress. The increasingly massive doses of Arab, Leftist, and isolationist propaganda make it necessary for
Jews to argue the case for Israel before all the American
people. We must train speakers in every community to
speak before service clubs, church groups, schools, and the
like, so as to explain why American support of Israel is
politically and militarily in the American interest as well as
morally obligatory. Should you be a member of any such
organization, arrange to have someone speak on behalf of
Israel. Richard Reeves, a non-Jewish journalist (writing in
New York magazine, December 23, 1974) criticized American Jewry for confining its pro-Israel efforts to Washington and a few centers of Jewish population. The time has

come for "American Jews . . . to take the offensive and argue the merits of their case for Israel without apology or self-pity." Unless we organize popular American support for Israel, congressmen monitoring the feelings of their constituents will begin to weaken in their support of Israel.

3. Support political candidates who show concern for Israel and other Jewish and moral issues. This support should not only be in money, but in volunteer and other work. Seeking out candidates who want to see a living and healthy Israel does not raise an issue of dual loyalty. Any candidate who advocates withdrawing American support from the only democracy in the Middle East conflict is certainly not morally worthy of political office in this democracy.

4. Give money. Give to the United Jewish Appeal, Israel Bonds and other Israeli causes. American Jews have responded generously in the past (though the sad fact is that more than half of the Jews in the United States have never given to Israel), but the continuing crisis situation in Israel necessitates our responding even more generously in the future. Until now, we have met few Jews who had to forego vacations or postpone purchases because of their contributions to Israel. But with the current recession in the United States it is possible that giving to Israel will require some people to sacrifice certain luxuries. This will be painful, but it must be done. Tzedaka is not charity; it is justice.

Part 4

SOVIET JEWRY

In Jewish law the commandment to redeem captives is so important that we must sell synagogue buildings and even Torah scrolls, if necessary, to raise the needed money. Nevertheless, the major American Jewish organizations' annual budget for publicity and protest on behalf of Soviet Jewry is less than half a million dollars. While Jewish law demands that we stand ready to sell synagogues and Torah scrolls, American Jewry allocates (an allocation which is itself the result of long and intense internal pressure by a handful of committed people) a sum that is less than the cost of a modern synagogue building.

There are, however, a number of independent groups working on behalf of Soviet Jews which have been doing extraordinarily important work. The reader is asked to contact one or more of them.

The pioneer, and still indispensable group, is the New York based Student Struggle for Soviet Jewry and Center for Russian Jewry, headed by Jacob Birnbaum and Glenn Richter, two modern saints. Both of us, having travelled to Russia and worked for Soviet Jewry, can testify that though its yearly budget is under $100,000 this group organizes demonstrations whenever needed, co-ordinates the telephone calls to Russia that keep Soviet Jews and us informed, organizes Soviet Jewry activities throughout the United States, and serves as the most reliable source of information on the current situation of individual Soviet Jews.

Another extremely important group is the Union of Councils for Soviet Jews with chapters throughout the United States. The Union also operates on small sums of money while consistently, and successfully, developing programs and ideas to popularize the cause of Soviet Jewry.

It is also imperative that you work within any national Jewish organizations of which you are a member to insure that they play an active role within the National Conference on Soviet Jewry and, in the metropolitan New York area, in the Greater New York Conference on Soviet Jewry.

To become involved in Soviet Jewry work you should contact these organizations. Their addresses are listed at the conclusion of this section. Meanwhile, here are some suggested activities with which to begin.

1. Political Pressure

Support political candidates who show concern for Soviet Jewry; and express your gratitude to leaders in the movement to guarantee free emigration from the Soviet Union—men such as Senator Henry Jackson. Write letters to your elected officials expressing your concern for Soviet Jewry. If you do not, no one will. Also speak to non-Jewish friends about the issue and ask for their support in the struggle for free emigration from, and religious freedom in, the Soviet Union.

2. Correspond with Soviet Jews

Correspondence with Soviet Jews is an activity appropriate for both individuals and groups. You must first obtain from the groups mentioned above a list of current addresses of Soviet Jews wishing to leave. Then, simply start a program of regular writing to some of these people. It is impossible to exaggerate the importance of this simple activity. When I (J.T.) was in Novosibirsk, Central Siberia, in October, 1973, a local Jew, Isaac Poltinnikov, showed me his proudest possession—one hundred letters he had received from five continents and from more than

fifteen states throughout the United States. Dr. Poltinnikov has been without work for the three years since he
and his family applied for a visa, and he, his wife Irma, and
his daughter Victoria have been subject to terrible harassment and pressure. The correspondence provides him with
time-filling activities and assures him—and very importantly, assures other Jews who know about his case and
may consider applying to leave—that though inside
his country it appears that he is despised, overseas there
are people who do all that they can for him.

Letter writing, to be effective, must be regular. It is
very disconcerting for a Soviet Jew to receive a letter,
write a response, and never receive a reply. It is also important that all letters be sent by registered mail with
return receipt requested. This increases the cost of the
letter fourfold, but it is our only hope that the letter will be
delivered and not conveniently lost by Soviet postal authorities.

Bear in mind too that aside from boosting the morale of
the Soviet Jew who receives correspondence from abroad,
the volume of mail that comes to this person from abroad
puts the Soviet government on notice that the case of this
Jew is internationally known, and that any harassment of
him will be publicized. Such publicity saves lives.

3. Adopt a Family

There are a number of steps involved in adopting a
Soviet Jewish family. First, contact the Student Struggle
for Soviet Jewry for the name of a Soviet Jewish family in
need of assistance. S.S.S.J. will tell you the type of letters
to write, the type of packages to send, whether money can
be sent, whether it is wise to try to telephone the family,
and the types of political pressure you can exert on this
family's behalf. Such work provides physical and psychological assistance to the people in need, and the rela-

tionship that is formed can continue for a lifetime. Should these Soviet Jews succeed in emigrating to Israel, you can easily stay in touch with them there.

Because the adoption of a family involves much money and effort, it is an activity that is particularly appropriate for women's groups, clubs, youth groups, and the like.

4. Organize Demonstrations

A number of years ago, a Soviet official was overheard to remark at the United Nations, "Why should we change our policy towards the Russian Jews? We have promoted this policy for over fifty years while they (American and international Jewry) have been demonstrating for just a few. And we will be around long after their demonstrations have stopped." The job of world Jewry is to convince the Soviets that our demonstrations will not stop so long as Jews are forcibly confined to living in a country they want to leave. Whenever Soviet representatives gather, we must be there to remind them that we have not forgotten their victims; and we must hold this attitude with regard to Soviet artists as well as Soviet politicians. Should the Bolshoi, for example, visit any country where Jews are free, we must greet them with leaflets and other forms of protest. We have nothing against these artists, nor against art. But we know that the Soviets do not see art as a value in itself; and we know that when these performers return home, the Soviet government analyzes the political repercussions of their trip. If it is reported that in every city the artists visited, people protested, the Soviets may become convinced—as indeed they have in the last few years—that unless they treat Soviet Jews in a civilized manner and allow them to leave, the Soviet name will be continually darkened. Thus, protests must continue even though 80,000 Jews have already left. For it is certain that if we weaken our efforts for Soviet Jews, soon none of them will be allowed to leave and their situation will have deteriorated to what it was when the protest movement started a decade ago.

Finally, remember that demonstrations are for the whole Jewish community. Never forget that the two Jews sentenced to death in Leningrad in December 1970 would have been murdered if not for demonstrations and protests. Demonstrations and protests work. Without them, Sylva Zalmanson would be in a prison camp, if not in her grave, rather than in Israel, and tens of thousands of Jews who emigrated would still be in the Soviet Union. Demonstrations are therefore not only "for kids" unless, of course, only kids care.

5. Symbolic Observances

Soviet Jewry must be an issue of constant concern to us. A Hasidic rebbe once remarked that just as a Torah scroll becomes invalid if only one letter is missing, so too the community of Israel becomes in a sense invalid when any Jew is missing from the community. The issue of Soviet Jewry must therefore be raised on all appropriate occasions, such as the Passover *seder* of freedom. It is important for us to constantly remember that only thirty years after a third of the Jewish people was extinguished, another fifth is in danger of disappearing.

Addresses of Soviet Jewry Organizations

1. Student Struggle for Soviet Jewry and
       the Center for Russian Jewry
    200 West 72nd Street
    New York, New York 10023

2. Union of Councils for Soviet Jews
   1100 Seventeenth Street, N.E.-Suite 1000
   Washington, D.C. 20036

Union chapters throughout the United States:

   Arizona Council on Soviet Jewry
   Southern California Council for Soviet Jews
   Orange County Commission on Soviet Jews
   California Students for Soviet Jews
   San Diego Council for Soviet Jewry
   Soviet Jewry Action Group
   Cleveland Council and Soviet Anti-Semitism
   Chicago Student Struggle for Soviet Jewry
   Long Island Committee for Soviet Jewry
   Toronto Council for Soviet Jews
   Pittsburgh Voice for Soviet Jewry
   Cincinnati Council for Soviet Jewry
   Niagara Frontier Council for Soviet Jewry
   Washington Committee for Soviet Jewry
   South Florida Conference on Soviet Jewry
   Greater Philadelphia Council for Soviet Jews
   Montreal Student Struggle for Soviet Jews
   Zechor-S.E. Virginia Council for Soviet Jews

3. National Conference on Soviet Jewry
   11 West 42nd Street
   New York, New York 10036

4. Greater New York Conference on Soviet Jewry
   11 West 42nd Street
   New York, New York 10036

Part 5

LASHON HA-RAH

The Hafetz Hayyim, a great Lithuanian Jewish scholar of the nineteenth and twentieth centuries, and a leader of Eastern European Jewry, would exact a promise from rabbis that they would be as careful to refrain from gossiping and slandering as they were not to eat pork.

Tenuat Ha-Musar *by Dov Katz, Tel Aviv: 1967, Vol. 4 p. 148*

Lashon Ha-Rah
(gossip when true, slander when false)

There is a Hassidic tale about a man who went through his community slandering the rabbi until one day, feeling remorseful, he begged the rabbi for forgiveness, and indicated that he was willing to undergo any penance to make amends. The rabbi told him to take several feather pillows from his home, cut them open and scatter the feathers to the winds. The man did so immediately, and returned to the rabbi to notify him that he had fulfilled his request. The rabbi then told him, "Now go and gather all the feathers that the wind has scattered. For though you are sincerely remorseful and truly desirous of correcting the evil which you have done, it is about as possible to repair the damage done by your words as it will be to recover the feathers" (retold in Hayim Donin's *To Be A Jew*).

This story vividly illustrates the irreparable damage done by gossiping. Yet despite its terrible effects, *lashon ha-rah* is an offense that almost everyone commits every day.

Consider the following laws of the Torah:

Leviticus 19:16: "Do not go about as a talebearer among your people." The word in Hebrew for talebearer corresponds to the word for peddler, the implication being that just as a peddler goes from house to house buying from one and selling to another, so does the gossiper. There is a peddling mentality to the gossiper. When we tell someone something very intimate about a third party (something we might even have been told in confidence), we expect to be told something in return of equal intimacy about someone else. We peddle one intimacy off for another.

Leviticus: 19:14, 17: The Hafetz Hayying wrote a *two hundred page volume* based on Jewish sources just outlining the seriousness of the sin of gossiping. In the introduction to the work, the author notes that in addition to the prohibition against talebearing, we violate other Torah precepts when we listen to gossip. *Leviticus* 19:14 informs us, "You shall not place a stumbling block before a blind man." The Hafetz Hayyim explains that by providing an audience for a gossiper, you are making it possible for him to indulge in this sinful act and to stumble morally. Furthermore, if you gossip about someone behind his back while pretending to be a loyal friend, besides being a hypocrite, you are violating yet another commandment, "You shall not hate your brother in your heart" (*Leviticus* 19:17). As Norman Lamm writes concerning the Hafetz Hayyim's citation of the Biblical verses gossipers and listeners violate, "This is not a matter of piling up violations in order to show the author's legal virtuosity or to impress the pious reader. It is a bold act of stripping an accepted social convention in order to reveal the enormity of the evil it begets and its dreadful consequences" (*The Good Society*, selected and edited by Norman Lamm, New York: 1974).

To start acting Jewish in this realm, we suggest: Start

eliminating gossip entirely at certain times, e.g., the Friday night Shabbat meal. At this lengthy meal make it a point to speak about *issues rather than personalities*. The more difficult you find this is to accomplish, the better you will know how much you need intellectual, spiritual and moral growth. For gossiping about others usually reveals two things: a sense of inferiority which can be assuaged only when all others are shown to be at a correspondingly low level, and a mind that is incapable of, or not used to, thinking abstractly and productively.

—Try to avoid as much as possible spending time with people who gossip. Either choose the company of people from whose conversation you will learn, or, if you cannot avoid being with gossips, try to change the topic. If necessary, tell them why you are doing so. Don't be offensive, but if it is unavoidable, offend them. It is better to offend the perpetrators of the gossip than to conspire in destroying people whose private lives are being dissected. Besides, in all likelihood you too will soon become a victim of these gossips.

If you find that your friends rely on gossiping for the bulk of their conversation, you may want to qualitatively increase—even at the price of numerically decreasing—your circle of friends. In choosing friends, the most effective guideline is to choose people from whom you can learn (character traits as well as ideas and facts).

—As we mentioned earlier, just as one should not gossip himself, one is forbidden to encourage others to gossip. Therefore, friends should not ask each other to reveal the contents of intimate conversations and private affairs, and likewise parents should not encourage their children to tell them everything concerning their friends or their friends' parents.

The next time you find yourself talking about others,

remember this insight of Israel Salanter, the great Jewish moralist and rabbinic teacher of the last century. Salanter noted that we usually confuse our priorities. *Normally,* Salanter said, *we worry about our own material well-being and our neighbor's souls; let us rather worry about our neighbor's material well-being and our own souls.*

Part 6

BLESSINGS, PRAYERS AND TEFILLIN

"Blessings were instituted by the Rabbis as a means for directing man into the presence of God at all times, thus providing for the continuous preservation of contact with the Creator" (Pinchas Peli, "Blessings—The Gateway to Prayer," *Tradition*, Fall, 1973, p. 65). Abraham Heschel has noted that when we drink a glass of water "we remind ourselves of the eternal mystery of creation, 'Blessed be Thou . . . by whose word all things come into being.' A trivial act and a reference to the supreme miracle. Wishing to eat bread or fruit, to enjoy a pleasant fragrance or a cup of wine: . . . on noticing trees when they blossom; on meeting a sage in Torah or in secular learning . . . we are taught to invoke His great name and our awareness of Him. . . . This is one of the goals of the Jewish way of living: to experience commonplace deeds as spiritual adventures; to feel the hidden love and wisdom in all things" (*God in Search of Man*, New York: 1955, pp. 45-50).

For the Jew who accustoms himself to making blessings, there is a continuous sense of the mystery and grandeur of existence as well as a constant affirmation that we do not own the world but merely serve as its custodians. Blessings insure that religion is an active force in the life of the individual at all times, not just on selected holy days.

The most convenient place to find the *berakhot* (blessings) is in a Siddur (prayerbook). The Siddur is a sort of mini-encyclopedia of Jewish life. As Hayim Donin has written: "The Siddur is study as well as prayer. It is moral instruction and ethical guidance as well as pleas for personal needs. It emphasizes *man's duties as well as his rights*" (*To Be A Jew*, New York: Basic Books, 1972, p.

177

180). Probably the most useful Siddur in English is the edition edited and translated by Philip Birnbaum (New York: Hebrew Publishing Company). Birnbaum's Siddur contains the Hebrew text, a readable English translation, and insightful notes scattered throughout the volume.

Some suggestions:

Start all meals with the *hamotzi*—the blessing over bread: "Blessed are You, Lord our God, King of the Universe, who brings forth bread from the earth." Also try to learn the *Birkat Hamazon* (the grace after meals) and accustom yourself to saying at least some of the blessings. Though it is, of course, permissible to say prayers in any language it is infinitely preferable to know the Siddur in its original language.

Develop the habit of starting the day with prayer. As we have written, *l'hitpallel* (to pray) literally means to judge oneself; and what better way to start each morning than with a few minutes of self-judgment and introspection before God? An integral part of the morning prayer service for the Jew is the donning of Tefillin (phylacteries) opposite the heart and mind. One who puts on Tefillin gives his day a spiritual dimension. Consider the experience of the great sculptor, Jacques Lipchutz. Lipchutz a non-observant Jew, was advised late in his life by the Lubavitcher Rebbe to start wearing Tefillin. Lipchutz described the effect of this religious act as follows: "I daven (pray) every morning. It is of great help to me. First of all, it puts me together with all my people. I am with them. And I am near to the Lord, the Almighty, I speak with Him. I cannot make any prayers individual, but I speak to Him. He gives me strength for the day. . . . I could not live any more without it" (*Reconstructionist*, February 1974 p. 20).

Part 7

TZEDAKA

"Everything in God's creation has a purpose" a Hasidic rebbe once told his disciples. "In that case," asked a disciple, "what then is the purpose of heresy, of denying that God exists?" "Apikorsus (heresy) is indeed purposeful," the rebbe replied, "for when you confront another who is in need, you should imagine that there is no God to help, but that you alone can meet the man's needs."

Tzedaka (inaccurately translated as charity)

Tzedaka means justice plus compassion. It is the feminine form of the masculine *tzedek*, which means justice. It is therefore quite dissimilar from its English equivalent "charity," a word which implies a generous deed beyond the call of duty. When one gives charity he is considered a charitable person, and when he does not, he is considered, at worst, selfish. In Judaism, however, tzedaka is an act of justice, so if one does not give Tzedaka he has committed an act of injustice.

The Torah legislated Tzedaka over 3,000 years ago. It legislated that every seventh year all the people would have equal access to the land; that the owner of the land could not take all the produce for himself, and that he was even forbidden to decide which poor people (such as relatives or friends) would receive it (*Leviticus* 25:1-7); that every third year one put aside a tenth of one's income for the poor, and that during the other two years, at harvest time, ("When you reap the harvest for your field, you shall not reap your field to its very edge, nor shall you gather the stray ears of corn. Likewise, you shall not pick your vineyard bare, nor gather up the grapes that have fallen. You shall leave these for the poor and the stranger" (*Leviticus* 19:9-10).

What must be appreciated here is not merely the Bible's humaneness but the extent to which Judaism felt it necessary to legislate selfless actions such as giving away one's property.

See Appendix A for examples of Judaism's systematic ethics with regard to Tzedaka.

Part 8

LEARNING ABOUT JUDAISM

According to the *Ethics of the Fathers* (2:5) "an ignorant person cannot be a pious person." This is not because an ignorant person necessarily lacks the desire to do good, but because doing good requires more than desire. To do good one must know what good is and how to distinguish it from evil. In order to act Jewish, one must know what Judaism is and what it demands. The following is a reading and study guide which should enable you to start learning what it means to be a Jew. The books represent various religious and scholarly approaches to Judaism, and bibliographical information on the books is appended.

The Bible

The basic source with which to start studying Judaism is, of course, the Bible, the most influential book in history. It has three sections: Torah (Teachings), Neviim (Prophets) and Ketuvim (Writings), and together they are known as the *TaNaKh*. Because of the Torah's importance and centrality—it is, one might say, the constitution of the Jewish people—it is read through every year in synagogue in fifty-two weekly portions. But one should not wait until the reading in synagogue to study the Torah, since the portion is read there quite rapidly, and in many congregations not in its entirety. An appreciation of the Torah necessitates systematic study individually and/or in groups. For study purposes there are available in English several excellent books about, and translations of, the Torah. The most readable translation is the 1962 version by the Jewish Publication Society, but it does not contain any commentary or discussion on the text. Highly recommended, therefore, is the Hertz Chumash which in addition to the 1917 JPS translations includes an accompanying commentary by the late Chief Rabbi of England, Joseph Hertz, which provides a summary of many of the traditional Jewish commentators, plus an analysis of the text with Rabbi Hertz' own religious-ethical insights. The Hertz Chumash belongs in every home.

For one wishing a deeper analysis of the philosophical, religious, and other issues raised in the weekly portion of the Torah, many of the brilliant writings of Nechama Leibowitz are now available in English. In each portion Dr. Leibowitz deals with a different concept and cites ideas from throughout Jewish literature (with occasional references to non-Jewish analyses of the Biblical text as well).

A superb guide which sets the first book of the Bible in its historical setting, and incorporates contemporary Biblical scholarship is *Understanding Genesis* by Professor Nahum Sarna of Brandeis University. Sarna utilizes modern scholarship and archaeology to deepen the significance of the Biblical texts, and few scholarly books give the reader as deep an appreciation of the ethical and philosophical profundities of the Torah, or of its originality.

For the rest of the Bible, (the *Nakh*), the most useful set to acquire is the *Soncino Books of the Bible*. They provide the Hebrew text, an English translation, and a fairly comprehensive commentary. To better understand the makeup, motivation, and general message of the Prophets, we also recommend Abraham J. Heschel's *The Prophets*.

A scholarly and readable analysis on the Biblical period, the origins of Judaism, and a scholarly Jewish response to many of the Biblical critics is Yehezkel Kaufman's classic *The Religion of Israel* as translated and condensed by Moshe Greenberg. Professor Kaufman, considered by many to be the greatest Jewish Biblical scholar of this century, makes a convincing case for the great antiquity and complete originality of the Jewish Bible and religion. This is an extremely important book, but for those who do not have the time or inclination to read in its entirety there is a summary of some of Kaufman's work by Kaufman himself in Leo Schwarz's *Great Ages and Ideas of the Jewish People.*

The Talmud and Jewish Law

The Talmud has been one of the most controversial books in history, and on at least 15 occasions in the last thousand years opponents of Judaism (the Church in particular) have had this work publicly burned. Throughout their history Jews made great personal sacrifices to preserve the Talmud. Rabbi Yechiel of Paris declared before Queen Blanche in 1240, "We are prepared to die for the Talmud. . . . Our bodies are in your power, but not our souls."

But the glorious and tragic history of the Talmud becomes far less glorious and even more tragic when we consider to what extent the great majority of contemporary Jews are ignorant of the contents of this work. Any beginning program of Jewish study must, therefore, include a basic overview of the Talmud.

Such an introduction to Talmudic literature is contained in Louis Jacobs' *Jewish Law*, which includes thirty-one selections from the Talmud, codes of Jewish law, and responsa literature, all accompanied by an excellent running commentary by Jacobs. Representative samplings of the engrossing non-legal *aggadic* (legendary and ethical) portions of the Talmud are compiled in the recently republished *A Rabbinic Anthology* by C.G. Montefiore and H. Loewe. A summary of Talmudic thought on many issues is contained in A. Cohen's *Everymans Talmud*, while George Horowitz's *The Spirit of Jewish Law* is a detailed 800-page overview of Jewish law in many different areas.

The Mishnah, the earliest written compilation of the oral

law, is available in two English translations. One, by Herbert Danby, is a one volume translation of the text with no commentary. The other, by Philip Blackman, is six volumes and, in addition to the textual translation, includes notes that cite the Biblical verses which are the basis for the Mishnaic law and explain the meaning and significance of all the terms used by the Mishnah.

In the centuries after the Mishnah was edited (around 200 C.E.) there arose a large body of literature, the Talmud, commenting on the Mishnah (you may have a clearer idea of the relationship of this material to the Mishnah if you compare the Mishnah to the American Constitution and the Talmud to the Supreme Court cases which ruled on the contemporary meaning and relevance of the Constitution). Eventually this body of literature was codified into two major works, the Jerusalem (or Palestine) Talmud and the Babylonian Talmud. For a variety of reasons the Babylonian Talmud emerged as the dominant work, so that in general, references to the Talmud are to the Babylonian Talmud. Fortunately, a number of recently published works in English make it now possible for anyone to learn the Talmud. The most exciting of these works is currently being published in Israel; it is a translation of the Talmud called the *El-Am Talmud*, edited by A. Ehrman and others. Sections of three tractates of the Talmud, *Berakhot* (blessings) *Kiddushin* (marriage) and *Bava Mezia* (civil claims), are currently available. Accompanying the translation is an extensive commentary which explains the Talmudic terms and places the Talmud in its historical setting. There has also been available for almost forty years the scholarly translation by Soncino Press of the entire Babylonian Talmud.

Jewish History
Many Jews express pride in Jewish history though they

know almost nothing about it. This is another Jewish tragedy, especially when one considers the excitement and significance of Jewish history.

We will of necessity confine our suggestions to a few popularly written but scholarly books on Jewish history. Hopefully, these books with their more extensive bibliographies will constitute an introduction to further reading in Jewish history.

In *Great Ages and Ideas of the Jewish People* Leo Schwarz gathered some of the greatest Jewish (and one non-Jewish) scholars of the twentieth century to write assessments of the period of Jewish history in which they specialized, such as the Biblical Age. the Talmudic period, the medieval Jewish world and the modern period. In terms of interest and information this book is the finest one-volume history of the Jews.

Louis Finkelstein's *The Jews* is another anthology of scholarly essays, and it is currently available in a three volume paperback edition. As evidenced by the sub-titles of the three volumes—"Their History," "Their Role In Civilization," "Their Religion and Culture"—the scope of Finkelstein's work is broader than Schwarz's; and many of the essays are masterpieces.

There are a number of good introductions to modern Jewish history, the period in which most contemporary Jews are interested. Howard Morley Sachar's *The Course of Modern Jewish History* conveys extensive information on the emancipation of the Jews and their entry into the modern world. The book, a one-volume encyclopedia of modern Jewish history, is excellent on most aspects of modern Jewish history, though weak on developments within Judaism. For an overview of Jewish religious history and thought in the past two centuries we recommend Joseph Blau's *Modern Varieties of Judaism*. The book is a fine introduction to the Reform, Conservative and Neo-Orthodox movements, but, as it is based on six lectures Blau delivered at universities in the United States, it is not a truly comprehensive work. A study of what has perhaps been the most dynamic movement in modern Jewish life, Zionism, is provided in Arthur Hertzberg's *The Zionist Idea*. In addition to a brilliant one hundred page introduction by Hertzberg, the book contains the most important writings of the leading Zionist thinkers.

For an American Jew wishing to better understand his own roots (which for most of us are Eastern European) an excellent anthology describing what life was really like in Eastern Europe is *The Golden Tradition*, edited by Lucy Davidowicz. Davidowicz has selected writings of Jews from all walks of life. The selections, often quite poignant, convey the sense of what it meant to be a Jew in eighteenth to twentieth century Poland and Russia. As for the development of Jewish life in America, Nathan Glazer's short but suggestive *American Judaism* is recommended.

We would again emphasize that almost all of the books mentioned have extensive bibliographies for further reading.

Some of the best writing about the history and makeup of the modern Jew is contained in novels. One such work is Milton Steinberg's *As A Driven Leaf*, a novel about Elisha ben Abuyah, the one teacher of the Talmudic period who became an apostate. The novel explores the tensions and dilemna of a Jew who rejects Judaism on intellectual grounds but ultimately finds that he is even more estranged, on moral grounds, from the non-Jewish world. Another novel which conveys at least as much truth as any non-fiction work on its subject is Elie Wiesel's *Night*, a shattering novel based on Wiesel's holocaust experience. A third novel, Isaac Bashevis Singer's *The Slave*, illuminates the dark period of the Chmelnitzky pogroms of 1648 (in which a third of European Jewry was destroyed), and as a

friend recently noted, is among the best *musar*, religious-
moral, books we have.

Jewish Thought

1) We enthusiastically recommend any book or article by
Eliezer Berkovits. Though in his mid-sixties, Berkovits, a
professor of Jewish Philosophy at the Hebrew Theological
College (outside Chicago), may well be the most challenging and revolutionary thinker in the Orthodox and general
Jewish community today. His writings are rational yet impassioned, scholarly yet accessible. Particularly important
are his recently published *Faith After the Holocaust*, his
profound reflections on Judaism and Jewish history in *God,
Man, and History*, and his steady stream of writings on
contemporary Jewish issues usually appearing in *Judaism*
and *Tradition* magazines.

2) Louis Jacobs is a man who writes books that have
deceptively simple titles, for his books reveal an incredible
erudition in almost all areas of Jewish knowledge. To read
through Jacobs' footnotes and bibliographies is simultane-
ously an exhilarating and depressing experience. Jacobs has
the ability to deal with themes that have been dealt with
countless times before, as in his book *Jewish Values*, and
through his vast erudition to give these topics freshness
and excitement. His *Principles of the Jewish Faith*, an
attempt to extract the enduring relevance of Maimonides'
Thirteen Principles of the Jewish Faith, is a masterful
overview of Jewish scholarship over the last two
hundred years, and his four volumes of anthologies of
*Jewish Law, Jewish Ethics, Philosophy and Mysticism,
Jewish Thought Today*, and *Jewish Biblical Exegesis* are
all excellent for high-school, university and adult study

3) American Jewry has much reason to be grateful to
Milton Himmelfarb. His informed and critical assessments

of contemporary Jewish life and thought (appearing four times a year in *Commentary* magazine) are important contributions to American Jewish enlightenment. Himmelfarb has performed another great service, however. In 1966 he invited 38 of the leading Conservative, Reform and Orthodox scholars in America to concisely describe their views on observance of Jewish law, the notion of Jewish chosenness, Jews and the "death of God," etc. The results of this effort are evident throughout our book, for we have taken a number of quotes from this anthology, *The Condition of Jewish Belief*.

4) Will Herberg's *Judaism and Modern Man* is a most profound exposition of the contemporary relevance of Judaism. Professor Herberg has vast acquaintance with general philosophy and political thought and every page is informed with his exciting scholarship. The book is not easy reading, but it is well worth the little extra effort needed.

5) Samuel Dresner's *The Jewish Dietary Laws* is a model of how an oft-discussed theme can be presented in a fresh, provocative and challenging manner. Dresner's discussion of Kashrut should be read both by Jews who observe Kashrut so as to insure that they understand the reasons for their practice, and by those who do not observe these laws so that they may come to appreciate the relevance and ethical importance of Kashrut. As Dresner writes, "other people engage in diets for their bodies. We have created a diet for the soul. If the first is understandable, why not the second?" At the end of Dresner's book is a short guide to keeping kosher by Seymour Siegel. Siegel presents the basic Halakhic guidelines of the Conservative movement, which differ in a number of major areas from Orthodox guidelines. One wishing an Orthodox guide to Kashrut should acquire the previously mentioned *To Be a Jew* by Hayim Donin, a basic outline of how to observe Jewish law today.

6) Herman Wouk's *This Is My God* is a moving account of why one man has made traditional Judaism the focus of his life and thought. Wouk, one of the leading novelists in America today, observes Jewish laws and spends at least one hour every day in study of the Talmud.

7) In 1953, a leading Zionist thinker, journalist, and activist died, and unfortunately with his death it appears that much of what he wrote was forgotten. Yet the contemporary reader who reads the Hayim Greenberg Anthology or the two volumes of Greenberg's *The Inner Eye* feels as if he has discovered a prophet. From his moral condemnation of Stalinism in the mid-1930's while many intellectuals stood in awe of the Soviet dictator, to his denunciation of the moral bankruptcy of the American Jewish leadership in 1943 for not doing anything substantial for European Jewry, to his 1951 criticism of the Zionists for stressing Zionism over Judaism, Hayim Greenberg wrote with the vision, ethical scope, love, and courage of a prophet.

8) Viktor Frankl's *Man's Search For Meaning* is perhaps the most important attempt to articulate a psychological world-view compatible with a religious approach. While acknowledging the significance of Freud and the sexual drive and Adler and the drive for power, Frankl sees as the determinative element in man the search for meaning. His analysis is particularly poignant because the story of his life is inextricably intertwined with the development of his theories. Much of Frankl's "logotherapy" evolved during the years he spent in Nazi concentration camps, and his work is a fascinating retelling of his experiences, coupled with a presentation of his views.

9) Trude Weiss-Rosmarin's *Judaism and Christianity-The Differences* is precisely what its title states, a presentation of the differences between the two religions. Anyone

familiar with Dr. Weiss-Rosmarin is acquainted with her rather vigorous writing style, and in this volume she states with clarity and scholarship what she sees as the decisive differences between Judaism and Christianity.

BIBLIOGRAPHY

The Bible
Editions of the Bible:
The Holy Scriptures According to the Masoretic Text. Philadelphia: JPS, 1917.
The Torah: The Five Books of Moses. Philadelphia: JPS, 1962.
Joseph Hertz, *The Pentateuch and Haftorahs.* London: Soncino Press, 1972.
The Soncino Books of the Bible. London: Soncino, 1950.

Abraham Joshua Heschel, *The Prophets.* Philadelphia: JPS, 1962.
Yehezkel Kaufman, *The Religion of Israel: From its Beginnings to the Babylonian Exile.* Chicago: University of Chicago Press, 1960; New York: Schocken paperback.
Nechama Leibowitz, *Studies in the Book of Genesis.* Jerusalem: World Zionist Organization, Department for Torah Education and Culture, 1972.
Nahum Sarna, *Understanding Genesis.* New York: McGraw-Hill, 1966; New York: Schoken Paperback.

Jewish Law
Phillip Blackman, *Mishnayoth,* New York: Judaica Press, 1964, in 6 vols.
A. Cohen, *Everyman's Talmud.* New York: Dutton, 1949.

Herbert Danby, *The Mishnah*. Oxford: Oxford University Press, 1933

A. Ehrman, ed. *The Talmud*. Jerusalem and Tel Aviv: El-Am-Hoza'a Leor Israel.

C.G. Montefiore and H. Loewe, *A Rabbinic Anthology* Philadelphia: JPS, 1960; Schocken paperback.

George Horowitz, *The Spirit of Jewish Law*. New York: Central Book Company, 1953.

Louis Jacobs, *Jewish Law*. New York: Behrman House, 1968.

The Talmud. London: Soncino Press, 1935.

Jewish History

Joseph Blau, *Modern Varieties of Judaism*. New York and London: Columbia University Press, 1964; also in paperback.

Lucy Davidowicz, ed. *The Golden Tradition*. New York: Holt Rineheart and Winston, 1967; Boston: Beacon paperback

Louis Finkelstein, ed. *The Jews: Their History, Culture and Religions*, 3 volumes. New York: Schocken paperback.

Nathan Glazer, *American Judaism*. Chicago: University of Chicago Press, 1957; also in paperback.

Arthur Hertzberg, *The Zionist Idea*. Garden City, New York: Doubleday, 1959; Philadelphia: JPS, paperback.

Howard Morley Sachar, *The Course of Modern Jewish History*. Cleveland: World, 1958. New York: Dell, paperback.

Leo Schwarz, ed. *Great Ages and Ideas of the Jewish People*. New York: Random House, 1965.

Historical Novels

I. Bashevis Singer, *The Slave*, New York: Avon paperback.

Milton Steinberg, *As A Driven Leaf*, New York: Behrman House, 1939; also in paperback.

Elie Wiesel, *Night*. New York: Hill and Wang, 1960; New York: Avon paperback.

Jewish Thought

Eliezer Berkovits,
> *God Man and History*. New York: Jonathan David, 1959;
> also in paperback
> *Faith After the Holocaust*. New York: Ktav Publishing
> House, Inc. 1973.

Hayim Donin, *To Be A Jew: A Guide to Jewish Observance in
Contemporary Life*. New York: Basic Books, 1972.

Samuel Dresner, *The Jewish Dietary Laws*. New York:
Burning Bush, 1959.

Viktor Frankl, *Man's Search for Meaning*. Rev. ed. Boston:
Beacon, 1963; New York: Washington Square Press,
Simon and Schuster, and others, paperback.

Hayim Greenberg,
> *The Inner Eye*. 2 vol. New York: Jewish Frontier Publish-
> ing Association, 1953, 1964.
> *The Hayim Greenberg Anthology*. Edited by Marie
> Syrkin, Detroit: Wayne State University Press, 1968;
> also in paperback.

Will Herberg, *Judaism and Modern Man*. Philadelphia:
JPS, 1951; New York: Atheneum, paperback.

Milton Himmelfarb, ed. *The Condition of Jewish Belief*. New
York: Macmillan, 1966; also in paperback, 1969.

Louis Jacobs,
> *Jewish Biblical Exegesis*. New York: Behrman House,
> 1973.
> *Jewish Ethics Philosophy and Mysticism*. New York:
> Behrman House, 1967.
> *Jewish Law*. New York: Behrman House, 1968.
> *Jewish Thought Today*. New York: Behrman House, 1970.
> *Jewish Values*. Hartford, Connecticut: Hartmore House,
> Inc., 1960.
> *Principles of the Jewish Faith*. New York: Basic Books,
> 1964.

Trude Weiss-Rosmarin, *Judaism and Christianity—The Differences*, New York: Jewish Book Club, 1943; New York: Jonathan David, paperback.

Herman Wouk, *This Is My God*. New York: Doubleday and Company, 1959; also in paperback.

Part 9

FINAL CONSIDERATIONS

A friend once suggested a simple test for a person to assess the vitality of his or her Jewishness. "Imagine you were being followed by someone for twenty-four hours—would any of your actions indicate to the shadow that you were a Jew?"

We think it fair to say that most American Jews, on any given day, would fail this test. In most American Jewish households, only if the shadow appeared on Rosh Ha-Shanah, Yom Kippur or one of the first nights of Passover would he know that he had been observing a Jew. But taking cognizance of one's Judaism on one, two, or three holidays a year is as impressive as showing respect to one's mother only on Mother's Day. Judaism is a value-shaping way of life, not a semi-annual ritual.

What then, in addition to our previous suggestions, can one do on any given day to live as a Jew? We offer some final suggestions to actualize the ideas of each of our questions and answers.

Question 1 (God): Strive to have your actions reflect two facts: that all human beings are created in the image of God, and that there is one standard of right and wrong which emanates from the one God.

Question 2 (Jewish Law): We have written of specific laws such as Shabbat, Kashrut, Mezuzzah, Tefillin, Lashon Ha-Rah, both in Question 2 and in this last answer. However, as Nachmanides pointed out (see p. 56), the guiding principle behind all the laws must be *kedoshim t'hiyu* "You shall [all] be holy" (Leviticus 19:2). To cite one example, there is no specific Jewish law concerning behavior at sports events, but a person constantly aware of *Leviticus*

194

19:2 will not be among the mob who cheer when hockey players beat each other up.*

Question 3 (Unethical Religious Jews and Ethical Irreligious People): As an observant Jew you are required to do two things. First, you must insure that Jews who make a mockery of God and the Jewish community by observing some of Judaism's laws while violating its ethical laws are denied any positions of leadership in the Jewish community, and are made aware of your displeasure at their conduct. Knowledgeable Jews must observe the Torah's law: "You shall reprove your fellow man [when you see him performing a wrong]" (*Leviticus* 19:16). If you belong to a synagogue where the rabbi conducts classes in Jewish texts, urge him to teach or review the laws dealing with business ethics and behavior.

Your second obligation as a committed Jew is to seek out the ethical irreligious person and explain to him how Judaism combines his ethical concerns with means to perpetuate his ethics. Remind him that as Jews we have a moral role to perform and the more people performing the role the stronger we—and ethics—are.

Question 5 (Jewish Role): Do what you can in your personal life to further the Jewish goal of "perfecting the world under the rule of God." Maimonides wrote that the ninth positive commandment of the Torah obliges the Jews ". . . to proclaim this true religion to the world, undeterred by fear of injury from any source."

Question 6 (Alienated Young Jews): Ask yourself and your children the question we were asked by teenagers in

---

*How is one to be constantly aware of this principle? Judaism legislated an ethical string-around-the-finger to remind one of one's obligations. It is called *tzizith*, the ritual fringes the Bible instructs us to wear so that "you will see it and remember all my commandments" (*Numbers* 15:39).

one town in Pennsylvania: "Can Hitler be called evil, or do we consider him evil because we don't like what he did?"

Ask yourself and your children the following question: If Judaism is just beautiful ethics why shouldn't a Jew marry a beautifully ethical Christian?

If you can't answer these questions, there is a good chance that you are raising your children in the only type of Judaism that you and they might ever know—caricatured Judaism.

Remember, you cannot rely on temple services to keep your children Jewish. You must create a Jewish home and insure that your children are learning experientially and intellectually at home and at school what it means to be a Jew. Check out the local Hebrew school—are your children learning Judaism or advanced spitball shooting and intermediate Lulav-shaking?

There exist in American Jewish life at least three extraordinarily effective institutions for introducing people to living Judaism.

For high school students, Yeshiva University sponsors "Torah Leadership Seminars," week-long retreats of intensive Jewish study, song, dance, rap sessions, and fun. These seminars have introduced thousands of young people to authentic and vibrant Judaism. Contact:

Torah Leadership Seminars
500 West 185th Street
New York, New York 10033

For young men and women between the ages of 18-26 the Brandeis Institute offers month-long programs each summer. Founded and directed by Dr. Shlomo Bardin, the summer institute is one of the most beautiful experiences (Jewish or otherwise) which a person can ever have, and it is one of the most effective programs anywhere for fostering love for Jewish life. The Institute is located on a vast expanse of land in beautiful Simi Valley about forty miles north of Los Angeles. The summer institute is ideal for instilling in young Jews with little or no background in Judaism Jewish values and feelings. During the rest of the year the Institute conducts introductory and advanced weekends for adults. We know of no comparable program: it has probably trained the majority of Reform and Conservative lay Jewish leaders on the West Coast (and many leaders in the rest of the country attended the summer institute as youths). For information contact:

Brandeis Institute
Brandeis, California 93064

An extraordinarily successful center of Jewish life on the East Coast is the Lincoln Square Synagogue, Steven Riskin, rabbi. Among the many activities of this congregation are the Joseph Shapiro Academy—an adult educational program with over thirty courses and more than 1,000 students, and active programs of *Shabbatonim* and outreach to the Jewish community of New York. For information on the Synagogue's many programs, contact:

Lincoln Square Synagogue
200 Amsterdam Avenue
New York, New York 10023

Question 7 (Intermarriage): You are a Jew because for 3500 years, Jews preceding you willed to be Jews, despite the dangers and hardships that they had to endure. Had a single one of your hundreds of ancestors left the Jewish community you would not today be a Jew. Therefore, before you give it up, you owe it to those hundreds of ancestors as well as to yourself to devote some time to a serious attempt to understand why those of us who have studied Judaism consider it the most powerful idea in history.

We have now come to the end of our attempt to answer just eight questions about Judaism. Probably the best general advice on how to act as a Jew was provided 2,000 years ago, in a tale that is often retold, about Hillel, a rabbi in Israel. A non-Jew once came to Hillel and asked him to define the essence of Judaism while standing on one leg. "What is hateful unto you, do not do unto your neighbor. The rest is commentary," the rabbi answered. Unfortunately people tend to end the story at this point and omit the final words of advice with which Hillel concluded his message. For Hillel then appended one more statement, without which the prior advice would be abstract and difficult to actualize in daily behavior. After defining the essence of Judaism, Hillel said to the non-Jew, in Aramaic, *zil g'mar* (go and study), which in Hebrew is **Tze Ulmad**. To you, our readers, we too conclude with the advice to **Tze Ulmad**.

The Tze Ulmad Institute and the authors welcome additional questions, answers, comments and suggestions from the readers of this book. We hope in this manner to encourage an international Jewish dialogue, and to start publishing the fruits of this dialogue in a new journal, *Tze Ulmad Review*.

Tzedaka

AN EXAMPLE OF
JUDAISM'S SYSTEMATIC ETHICS

Appendix A

Laws of Tzedaka

(Taken from the *Abridged Skulkhan 'Arukh* of Rabbi Solomon Ganzfried, translated by George Horowitz in *The Spirit of Jewish Law* (New York: Central Publishing Company, 1953) and reprinted with permission of the author.

1. It is an affirmative command to give *tzedakah* to the poor of Israel, as it is said, "Thou shalt surely open thy hand . . .' (Deut. 15:8), and it is said, '. . . that thy brother may live with thee' (Lev. 25:36). Anyone who sees a poor man begging alms and turns his glance away from him and does not give him *tzedakah* transgresses a negative command, as it is said, 'Thou shalt not harden thy heart nor shut thy hand from thy needy brother' (Deut. 15:7). *Tzedakah* is a mark of our descent from our father Abraham of whom it was said, 'For I have known him, that he may command his children . . .' (Gen. 18:9), i.e. to do charity . . .

. . . A man should also take to heart that life is like a revolving wheel, and in the end he or his son or his son's son may be reduced to taking *tzedakah*. He should not think, therefore, 'How shall I diminish my property in order to give to the poor.' Instead, he should realize that his property is not his own but only deposited with him in trust to do therewith as the Depositor (God) wishes . . .

2. Every person is obliged to give *tzedakah* according to his means, even a poor man who is supported by *tzedakah;* since he is permitted to take charity, even if he has a small sum of his own provided it is too little to produce an income sufficient to live on. In any event, since he has wherewith to sustain himself, he is obliged to give *tzedakah* out of what he receives. Even if he can give only a small thing, he should not hold back, for his little is considered the same as much from a rich man . . . Anyone, however, who has only enough for his bare subsistence is not obliged to give *tzedakah,* for one's own support comes before anyone else's.

3. How much does one give to a poor man? Sufficient to his need, but only to one who receives charity privately in secret. To him the people of the city should give all that he lacks in accordance with the standard he was accustomed to before he became impoverished. But to a poor man who goes begging from door to door one may give a small gift according to his dignity. In every city such persons should be given at least sufficient food for two meals per day and place to sleep. One should also feed and clothe the poor of idolators because of the ways of peace.

4. How much should one give as *tzedakah?* The first year a tenth of one's capital, and thereafter a tenth of one's gains each year. That is the middle way. It is most meritorious to give a fifth of capital the first year, and a fifth of gains thereafter. A person should not squander his substance, however, by giving away more than a fifth lest he himself become a public charge. This limit during one's lifetime, but at his death, a person may give up to a third of his wealth to *tzedakah.*

5. The tenth may not be used for general worthy purposes like candles for the synagogue or similar things, it must be given only to the poor. However, if the *mitzwah*

which one has occasion to perform is to officiate at a *berit* (circumcision) or to conduct a needy bride and groom to the *huppah* or the like or to buy books to lend to poor scholars to study from, he may use the money for such purposes. In the case of books, he must be careful to inscribe in them that they are dedicated to a public use so that his children may not acquire them by adverse possession.

6. If one gives to his grown sons and daughters . . . for whose support he is no longer responsible, so that the sons may study Torah and the daughters may conduct themselves properly; or makes gifts to his father whom he cannot support otherwise than out of funds intended for *tzedakah*, all such contributions are deemed *tzedakah*. Nay, more, he must prefer such persons to others, a needy relative to the other poor of his city, the poor of his own city to those of another place, as it is said: 'Thy poor and needy brother in thy land' (Deut. 15:11). But the communal collectors (*gabbayim* of *tzedaka*) should be careful not to favor their own needy kin more than other poor folk.

7. Any person who gives *tzedakah* with a disagreeable counterance and downcast mien, . . . transgresses the command: '. . . thy heart shall not be grieved when thou givest' (Deut. 15:10). He must give, instead, with a pleasant countenance and with joy, and must express sympathy for the poor man in his trouble, as Job said: 'If I have not wept for him that was in trouble and if my soul grieved not for the needy' (Job 30:25). He should speak words of consolation, as it is said: 'And I caused the widow's heart to sing'.

8. It is forbidden to turn back a poor man emptyhanded when he begs alms, even if one gives as little as a dried fig, as it is said: 'Let not the oppressed turn back in confusion' (Ps. 74:21). If one has nothing at all to give one should cheer him with words. It is forbidden to rebuke a poor man

or to raise one's voice and shout at him, for his heart is broken and crushed, as the Psalmist says: 'A broken and contrite heart thou wilt not despise.' Woe unto him who puts a poor man unto shame. One should be, instead, like a father to him both in compassion and in words, as it is said: 'I was a father to the needy' (Job 29:16).

12 The highest degree of *tzedakah*, beyond all others is to uphold a poor man before he is completely impoverished, to give him a substantial gift in a dignified manner to be used to earn a living, or to lend him a sum for that purpose, or to associate him in some venture or to procure for him some business or some work, in order to repair his fortunes so that he should not need help from others. That is meant by: '. . . thou shalt uphold him . . .' (Lev. 25:35), keep him so that he may not sink into utter destitution.

13 One should be careful to give the *tzedakah* as secretly as possible; and if it can be given in such a way that the donor does not know to whom he is giving and the recipient does not know from whom he is receiving, that is very good indeed.

15. One should always keep oneself far removed from taking *tzedakah*, and should suffer want rather than take assistance from others; for so commanded our Sages (their memory for a blessing): 'Make thy sabbath like a week-day, and do not require the help of others' (*Sabbath* 118). Even an honored scholar who becomes impoverished should exercise some craft, even an undignified one, rather than to require help from others.

16. Whoever should accept help because he is unable to sustain himself without it, due to illness, physical disability or old age and yet is too proud to accept; he is, indeed, a shedder of his own blood, and commits a mortal sin. He has for his suffering nothing but sin and transgression. Yet, whoever puts off as long as possible the taking of *tzedakah*

and suffers want, not out of pride, but rather in order not to burden the community, he will live to be a support of others. Regarding him Scripture says: 'Blessed is the man that trusteth in the Lord' (Jer. 17:7).

Appendix B

The following statement was circulated in February, 1975 by leading Orthodox Jews in the New York area. It is an example of religious Jewry's commitment to ethical behavior, and of the ability of ethical Jews to call unethical Jews to task on the basis of their shared commitment to Judaism.

"Critical challenges facing Jewry require communal solidarity. The moral stance of Jewish leaders and the trust they inspire affect solidarity. Jewish piety does not distinguish between ritual and ethics. We, the undersigned orthodox Jews, challenge Jewish—especially religious—leadership to restore high ethical standards to Jewish life. Since recurrent rumors and publicity alleging wrongdoing by Jews in leadership has brought no communal reform, we address this initial appeal to our associates and request endorsements, comments and similar initiatives from all our fellow counterparts.

"Any appearance of corruption or ethical cynicism is inconsistent with Jewish values. It threatens Judaism, weakens Jewish life, encourages anti-semites, and undermines support for Israel. Jewish honor has no price. Jewish leadership is a privilege demanding unquestionable probity. Those who want to lead us must meet Jewish standards (e.g., respect for the old, sick and poor, generous **tsedakah,** *moral compliance with law—Jewish and secular—denying honor to the dishonorable, refusing profit from impropriety, and ostracizing those who bring Judaism into disrepute). Public affairs may foster arrogance among the powerful and wealthy; but we insist that discredit to Jewish values disqualifies anyone from Jewish honors.*

"We serve notice on those who hesitate to give moral leadership: we will not permit our people, threatened outwardly to rot inwardly. We pledge to act in every area of our influence to apply scrupulous ethical standards, to oppose organization or leaders who tolerate corruption, and to reorder our Jewish house, with leaders deserving by Jewish standards of guiding us.

"As our first step, and without prejudice to legal presumptions of innocence, we 1) call upon any individual prominently identified with Jewish life in Israel or diaspora whose conduct or reputation reflects adversely on Jewish ethics to suspend himself from positions of Jewish leadership pending official exoneration; 2) admonish all Jewish organizations in Israel or diaspora—notably those speaking for orthodox Jews—to exonerate or suspend from membership anyone whose reputation discredits Judaism or Jews; and 3) urge all Jewish organizations in Israel or diaspora to enpower ethics committees to establish and maintain standards of conduct for their leaders by publication and responsible application of codes, and issuance of advice, warnings, chastisement and when necessary, disciplinary judgments.

"This statement, with your endorsements and comments (and those of your respected acquaintances), will be presented to appropriate Jewish leaders and organizations. We request suggestions for cooperative actions to pursue our principles in every area of Jewish life. Please reply promptly to Zedek, Apt. 161, 200 West 86th Street, New York, N.Y. 10024."

DENNIS PRAGER

For the last two years North American Jewry's most frequently engaged lecturer, Dennis Prager has a background of travel in 40 countries (including 7 Communist and 5 Arab), graduate work as a Fellow at the Columbia School of International Affairs and Russian Institute, a Yeshiva education, and the practical and theoretical study of alternate ways of life. He represented Jewry at the United Nations World Youth Assembly, was a U.S. delegate to the Brussels Conference on Soviet Jewry, and as National Spokesman for the Student Struggle for Soviet Jewry, was among the first to publicize the plight of Soviet Jewry.

A speaker of six languages, Mr. Prager, 26, has taught Jewish History and Religion at Brooklyn College and Political Science at Touro College. He has published articles on International and Jewish Affairs in *National Review, New Leader, American Zionist, Times Of Israel*, etc. In August, 1974, he served as scholar-in-residence at the Brandeis Institute in California, and during 1974-75 he is lecturing on this book and contemporary Jewish issues in five cross-continent lecture tours.

JOSEPH TELUSHKIN

Ordained in 1973 by Yeshiva University, Joseph Telushkin, 26, now divides his time between doctoral work in Jewish History at Columbia University and lecturing and conducting courses in Judaism and Jewish Affairs throughout the United States. Associate Director of the Tze Ulmad Institute, he has lectured in such far flung places as Japan, Australia, New Zealand, and Israel. During the Yom Kippur War he was in the Soviet Union, and was the first foreign Jew to meet with Jewish dissidents in Siberia. He also met with Soviet civil rights leader Andrei Sakharov. Mr. Telushkin has served as assistant to Professor Emil Fackenheim at the Hebrew University and teaches at the Shapiro Academy and Columbia Free Jewish University. He has written for *Tradition*, *Times Of Israel* as well as serving as Editor of *Yavneh Review*. In February 1975, he lectured on this book at an advanced seminar of the Brandeis Institute in California.

Prager and Telushkin first met eleven years ago in their second year at the Yeshiva of Flatbush High School in Brooklyn, New York. Eight years of countless theological and philosophical discussions later, they founded the Tze Ulmad Institute over corn muffins at four o'clock in the morning. The Institute's name means 'go and study,' and it now sends young Jews to lecture and conduct courses in Judaica around North America, prepares a dozen Jewish High School seniors to become future leaders in Jewish life, and has formed Tze Ulmad Press to publish and disseminate Jewish knowledge and ideas.

In February 1975, Prager and Telushkin conducted a course based upon this book at New York's 92nd Street YMHA.

February, 1975